Reprint

Analysis of Judas:
A Collection of
Archer Taylor's Articles on Judas Iscariot

"O Du Armer Judas"
Judas Iscariot in Charms and Incantations
The Judas Curse
The Gallows of Judas Iscariot
The Burning of Judas

Archer Taylor

Fathom Publishing Company

Introduction and images copyright © 2017 Ann Taylor Schwing. Reproduction or translation of any part of this work beyond that permitted by Section 107 or 108 of the 1976 United States Copyright Act without permission in writing from the copyright owner is unlawful. Requests for permission or further information should be addressed to the publisher.

ISBN: 978-1-888215-74-8
Library of Congress Control Number: 2017962270

"O Du Armer Judas" was first printed in Journal of English and Germanic Philology, Volume 19, Issue 3, July 1920.

Judas Iscariot in Charms and Incantations was first printed in Washington University Studies, Vol. VIII Humanistic Series, No. 1, 1920.

The Judas Curse was first printed in American Journal of Philology, Volume 42, Issue 3, 1921.

The Gallows of Judas Iscariot was first printed in Washington University Studies, Vol. IX, Humanistic Series, No. 2, 1922.

The Burning of Judas was first printed in Washington University Studies, Humanistic Series, Volume XI, No. 1, 1923.

Fathom Publishing Company
PO Box 200448
Anchorage, AK 99520-0448
www.fathompublishing.com
www.archertaylor.com

Archer Taylor

Archer Taylor (center) on an Atlantic cattle boat during a summer trip to Europe during his Swarthmore years.

Archer Taylor (left) with a friend and his sisters.

Introduction to Taylor Reprints

Archer Taylor was born August 1, 1890 and died September 30, 1973. He was called Archer because the family had difficulty agreeing on a name, and his uncle began calling him Sagittarius, symbolized in Greek mythology by the archer—half-man, half-horse in the ninth astrological sign.

Taylor wrote many books and a vast number of articles, some extended studies of the subject at hand and others short notes or queries. He grew up in a world in which academic-minded students learned Latin and Greek in grammar school, and he learned. In the years that followed, he continued to learn. Ultimately he read and spoke thirteen languages, with varying degrees of proficiency to be sure. In high school and early college years at Swarthmore, he worked on a cattle boat to Europe at the start of the summer. Once there, he traveled to the various countries in Europe learning the languages and meeting the people before returning to port to sign on a boat for the trip home. These experiences left him with a love of language and languages (and a life-long dislike for marmalade, pumpernickel and salt pork, the only foods for the crew on the voyage once the fresh things had been eaten). These experiences ended with World War I when he was caught in Europe at the start of the war and had to make his way home. His family sought news of his location and condition in the flyer shown on the next page.

After finishing Swarthmore in three years, Taylor taught and studied, earning his M.A. at the University of Pennsylvania and his PhD at Harvard and publishing his dissertation on the Wolfdietrich epics in 1915. He taught at Washington University in St. Louis starting in 1915, moving to the University of Chicago for the years 1925 into 1939. He ended his teaching career at the University of California, Berkeley, where he served from 1939 to 1958 and was chairman of the Department of German from 1940 to 1945. Taylor published *The Proverb* in 1931, followed by *Index to*

Mr. ARCHER TAYLOR, born August 1st, 1890, West Chester, Pennsylvania, U. S. of America, Father, American born Citizen, Lowndes Taylor, West Chester, Pennsylvania.

Instructor and Assistant Professor for two years at "State College" Pennsylvania.

Specialty, German Language and literature.

He went to Europe in June 1914, to persue special studies toward his Ph. D degree.

He was last heard from by postal mailed Wilhemlshohe, (Bz. Cassel) Germany.

In that postal he announced his intention to go at once to Gottingen.

He gave his address as "Archer Taylor, Dresden, Poste Restante, Germany.

But he has acknowledged no mail so addressed to him.

He has visited Germany several times on summer tours, and is somewhat familiar with the people and their language.

He speaks also a little French.

He is a graduate of Swarthmore College, a Quaker Institution, and also of the University of Pennsylvania.

He was studying at Harvard University for his Doctor's Degree, and went to Germany sssisted by Swarthmore College.

He had sufficient Credits for ordinary purposes and usual expenses in times of peace.

Please assist him in any way possible, also give any information of him to the German Police, and inform the local American Representatives, (Consul &c.)

Also kindly send information pegarding him to his uncle, Ervine D. York, Flushing, New York.

Or to his father,
Lowndes Taylor, West Chester, Pennsylvania,
U. S. of America.

the Proverb in 1934. His *Bibliography of Riddles* was published in 1939, and a number of other riddle books followed. Archer Taylor and Bartlett Jere Whiting published *A Dictionary of American Proverbs and Proverbial Phrases, 1820-1880* (Cambridge, Massachusetts: Harvard University Press 1958). Although much of his writing concerned folklore, he also wrote *A History of Bibliographies of Bibliographies* in 1955 and *General Subject-Indexes Since 1548* was published in 1966. Other books and an extraordinary number of articles flowed from his ongoing research, and these were the years before computers and word processing. My sister and I remember alphabetizing yellow 2x3 slips he prepared, one for each proverb or riddle.

Taylor married Alice Jones in 1915, and she bore him three children, Margaret, Richard and Cynthia. Alice sadly died early in 1930, and he married Hasseltine Byrd in 1932 and fathered two more children, Mary Constance and Ann.

A collateral benefit of his teaching position at the University of California was that Taylor could send his professional mail through the University. He carried on a prodigious correspondence with individuals and journals of similar interests around the world. When these individuals came to California, they often stopped to visit and to discuss their scholarship. Former students became close friends, illustrated by the friendship between Wayland Hand and Taylor that lasted the rest of Taylor's life. Many of Taylor's letters are collected at universities and some of the collections are available online.

His large library is now with the University of Georgia in Athens, except his ballad collection which is with the University of California, Berkeley. In addition to collecting books himself, Taylor watched for books and collections that he knew were sought by universities around the world. He might buy and send the desired books or notify the university so it could buy them. He was honored after World War II for his extended efforts to rebuild the university library in Dresden.

Wolfgang Meider published one of the reprints of *The Proverb* and posted a Biographical Sketch that included the following:

> In 1960 Archer Taylor was rightfully and deservedly honored by a most impressive "Festschrift" which his two friends Wayland D. Hand and Gustave O. Arlt edited with the befitting title *Humaniora, Essays in Literature, Folklore, Bibliography, Honoring Archer Taylor on His Seventieth Birthday* (Locust Valley/New York 1960). The subtitle summarizes Taylor's three major areas of expertise and such internationally renowned contributors as Bartlett Jere Whiting, L. L. Hammerich, Dag

Strömbeck, Stith Thompson, Walter Anderson, Taylor Starck, Kurt Ranke, Lutz Röhrich, Matti Kuusi, Georgios A. Megas, Robert Wildhaber, Francis Lee Utley, Anna Brigitta Rooth, Will-Erich Peuckert, Wolfram Eberhard, Julian Krzyzanowski, etc. acknowledge Taylor's worldwide influence.

Influenced by Wayland Hand, the Western States Folklore Society (formerly California Folklore Society) holds annual meetings to encourage professional and amateur folklorists to meet each other, present papers, and engage in discussions of all aspects of folklore and folklife. Since Taylor's 1973 death, the annual meeting has included the Archer Taylor Memorial Lecture. These lectures often reappear as scholarly articles, something that would have pleased Taylor.

Archer Taylor lived and died with friends around the world. He never passed up opportunities to explain and teach—the difference between anecdote and antidote, for example, when a teenage daughter got it wrong. He generously shared his knowledge and curiosity with all.

Ann Taylor Schwing
February 2018

Table of Contents

Introduction	v
"O Du Armer Judas"	1
Judas Iscariot in Charms and Incantations	23
The Judas Curse	38
The Gallows of Judas Iscariot	57
The Burning of Judas	79

"O DU ARMER JUDAS"

The German translation of the concluding strophe of a Latin Easter hymn, "Laus tibi, Christe, qui pateris":

> O tu miser Juda, quid fecisti,
> quod tu nostrum dominum tradidisti?
> ideo in inferno cruciaberis,
> Lucifero cum socius sociaberis.[1]

runs as follows:

> O du armer Judas,
> Was hast du getan,
> Dass du deinen herren
> Also verraten hast
> Darumb so mustu leiden
> Hellische pein,
> Lucifers geselle
> Mustu ewig sein.   Kyrieeleison.[2]

This German translation and parodies of it enjoyed a very remarkable popularity as satirical songs for several centuries, and the air is not yet forgotten in some parts of Austria.[3] It is particularly noteworthy as being "one of the few instances in which folk-song has borrowed a tune from the Church."[4]

---

[1] P. Wackernagel (*Das deutsche Kirchenlied*, I [Leipzig, 1864], 210, No. 347) gives the Latin text and its variants. W. Bäumker (*Das katholische deutsche Kirchenlied in seinen Singweisen*, I [Freiburg i. B., 1886], 462–463) adds nothing of importance on the Latin text.

[2] The text and music are conveniently accessible in Rochus, Freiherr von Liliencron, *Deutsches Leben im Volkslied um 1530* (*Deutsche National-Litteratur*, ed. J. Kürschner, XIII, Stuttgart, n.d.), pp. 227–228, No. 75 and elsewhere as cited below. The minor variations in the text are fully given by Wackernagel, *op. cit.*, II (Leipzig, 1867), 468–469, Nos. 616–618.

[3] The best study of the *Judaslied* is by R. Hildebrand in *Materialien zur Geschichte des deutschen Volksliedes, I: Das ältere Volkslied, Zeitschrift für den deutschen Unterricht*, Ergänzungsheft 5 to vol. XIV, Leipzig, 1900, pp. 63 ff. (I have not identified his citation "Monn., II, 281 ff.") See also Creizenach, "Judas Iscariot in Sage und Legende des Mittelalters," *Beiträge zur Geschichte der deutschen Sprache*, II (1876), 185–186 and Solovev, *K legendam ob Iudye predatelye*, Kharkov, 1898, pp. 116–117. Solovev cites Nordmeyer, "Pontius Pilatus in der Sage," *Beilage zur Allgemeinen Zeitung*, München, 22 April, 1895, 111, No. 92; but that article mentions Judas only in passing and is of no service here.

[4] F. M. Böhme. *Altdeutsches Liederbuch*, Leipzig, 1877, p. 646.

"O Du Armer Judas"

The date of the origin of this song is very uncertain. There seems to be no record of the melody much before 1400; and the earliest documentary evidence of its satirical employment is nearly a hundred years later. But, even though such songs may become popular very quickly, still the circumstances of its first recorded use seem to imply that it was known some time before the end of the 15th century. In fact there are passages which occur three or four hundred years earlier which may possibly contain allusions to the song. Müllenhoff suggests that the "armer Judas" of the song is referred to in the "Friedberger Christ und Antichrist," a fragmentary Old High German poem of the eleventh or twelfth century which narrates the life of Jesus und describes Antichrist and the Day of Judgment.[5] In describing the Last Supper the author says:

> bit demo brach er daz brôt
> demo armen Jude er iz bôt.

The use of the descriptive adjective "arm," *miser*, of Judas, and especially at the moment of his betrayal of his Master, is so unexpected that one is perhaps justified in thinking of the song. The editors of the *Denkmäler*, however, cite other and later instances[6] in which the same or a similar phrase appears, and it is therefore possible that the adjective is merely conventional, as in "der arme Sünder," and that its use here does not imply familiarity with the *Judaslied*.

[5] Müllenhoff and Scherer, *Denkmäler deutscher Poesie und Prosa aus dem VIII.-XII. Jahrhundert* (3rd ed. by E. Steinmeyer, Berlin, 1892), I, 102, No. XXXIII, C 11ª; see the notes, II, 197–201, especially p. 198.

[6] The following parallels are given: "den armen Judas er gebilidot" (*Ruland*, 70, 11); "der arme Judas" ("Urstende," K. A. Hahn, *Deutsche Gedichte der 12. und 13. Jahrhunderte*, 104, 69); "der ermiste man, von dem ich ie vernam, daz was Judas Scariotis" ("Leben Jesu," Hoffmann von Fallersleben, *Fundgruben*, I, 153, l. 31). Compare also
> Untriu, Nit dabî was,
> do der arme Jûdas
> den wâren gotes sun verriet
> benamen umb ein kleine miet

in Seifrid Helbling (ed. J. Seemüller, Halle, 1886, p. 244 [VII, 174]). For other curious uses of the word "arm" see Helbling, p. 271 (VII, 1013); p. 270 (VII, 980); *Wigamur*, v. 277; *Muspili*, v. 66 (cf. Müllenhoff and Scherer,[3] II, 34); Otfrid, I, 17, 51. Hildebrand (*Materialien*, p. 62, n. 3) remarks that the phrases "armer Teufel," "armer Schächer" are "certainly derived from the medieval stage."

Taylor

There is an interesting passage in Wolfram von Eschenbach's *Parzival*,[7] in which Bartsch thought he found a reminiscence of the Judas song:

> Unt der arme Jûdas,
> Der bî eime kusse was
> An der triuwenlosen vart,
> Da Iesûs verraten wart.

But Martin[8] considers the adjective a fixed epithet, which was perhaps suggested by a passage in *Brandan:*

> Ich bin ez der arme Judas
> der ie ungetriuwe was...[8a]

Solovev, moreover, finds an allusion to the *Judaslied* in the following lines from the *Klage* of Hartmann von Aue:

> Und daz diu arme sêle mîn
> Êwechlîchen müeze sîn
> In der tiefen helle
> Jûdases geselle,
> Dâ niemen fröude haben mac,
> Unz an den jungesten tac.[9]

Bech's note on this passage, however, makes it evident that the wish expressed here is a part of the medieval oath which employed the name of Judas and other notorious Biblical sinners for their terrifying effect.[10]

In the generation just preceding the Reformation we meet the first demonstrable allusion to the Judas song, and find that it was then utilized as a song of mockery. Emperor Maximilian caused the *Judaslied*, "carmen illud maledictionis,"[11] to be

---

[7] Ed. Lachmann, 219, 25 (Book IV, vv. 1212–1216); ed. Bartsch,² I (*Deutsche Klassiker des Mittelalters*, IX, Leipzig, 1875), p. 230; ed. E. Martin, I (*Germanistische Handbibliothek*, IX, 1, Halle a. S., 1900), p. 76.

[8] Vol. II (1903), *Kommentar*, p. 204, cf. Berichtigungen und Nachträge, p. xcvii.

[8a] Ed. Schröder, vv. 965–966. Martin's reference to v. 1351 is apparently incorrect. I see no reason for thinking that Wolfram was acquainted with these lines; the phrase "der arme Judas" as a commonplace.

[9] Vv. 1430 ff. (*Deutsche Klassiker des Mittelalters*, V, *Hartmann von Aue*, III, 3rd ed., Leipzig, 1891, p. 96).

[10] On this oath see H. Martin, "The Judas Iscariot Curse," *American Journal of Philology*, XXXVII (1916), 434–451 and my additions in a forthcoming number of the same journal.

[11] Liliencron (*Die historischen Volkslieder der Deutschen*, II [Leipzig, 1866], 184) quotes the phrase from Oefele, *Script.*, I, 224; cf. also Hildebrand, p. 63.

"O Du Armer Judas"

played when, on the 26th of May, 1490, he floated down the Danube past the defiant inhabitants of Regensburg. The city had renounced its allegiance to the Holy Roman Empire in 1486 and had turned to Bavaria, and, on the occasion of the Emperor's visit to that part of the Empire four years later, the rebellious citizens refused him admission.

Naturally so effective a weapon of satire was not neglected in the bitter strife which accompanied the Reformation, and in the two generations between 1520 and 1580 the Judas song was parodied repeatedly.[12] Perhaps its first employment for satirical purposes is that in the "Defensio Christianorum de Cruce, id est, Lutheranorum" of 1520, an attack on Murner, the cleverest and foulest of Luther's opponents. He had to endure this far from witty adaptation of the song:

> Ach du armer MURNarr,
> Was hastu getan,
> das du also blint
> in der heilgen schrift bist gan?
> des mustu in der kutten
> liden pin,
> aller gelerten MURR NARR
> mustu sin.
> Ohe ho lieber Murnar.[13]

And during the feuds which devastated Germany for the next generation, indeed for more than a century and a half, the *Judaslied* is heard again and again. In 1525 when the peasants withdrew from the Marienberg just outside of Würzburg, the watchman blew the tune to express his scorn of the retreating enemy:

> Da war ein groszes frohlocken und schreien im ganzen schlosz Marienberg; der thürner auf dem mittleren thurn blies den bauern das gemein liedlein: hat dich der schimpf gereuen, so zeug du wider heim.[14] So ward der fordere

---

[12] I do not find it mentioned in Kopp, "Die niederdeutschen Lieder des 16. Jahrhunderts," *Jahrbuch des Vereins für niederdeutsche Sprachforschung*, XXVI (1900), 1 ff., 32 ff.; nor in A. Hartmann, *Historische Lieder und Zeitgedichte vom 16. bis 19. Jahrhundert* (ed. H. Abele).

[13] Hoffmann von Fallersleben, *Geschichte des deutschen Kirchenliedes*, Hannover, 1861, p. 232. The "Defensio" was written by Matthäus Gnidius, see J. M. Lappenberg, *Dr. Thomas Murners Ulenspiegel*, Leipzig, 1854, p. 417.

[14] A song which is frequently referred to in the chronicles of this period, but which has not been preserved; see Hildebrand's interesting discussion, pp. 59 ff.

Taylor

thürner herab auf die schut geführt und blies den Wirzburgern den armen Judas: o Judas, armer Judas, ach was hastu getan.[15]

The ballad of Fritz Beck, master of ordnance for the besieged, reports this event with mention of the Judas song:

> Der thurner blies den Judas,
> ach was hast du gethan!
> es waren selzam laudes,
> es lacht nicht iederman.
> er blies: hats dich gerewet,
> so ziehe wider heim.[16]

Further south, in Switzerland, the Catholics played the song of Judas, the traitor, on the organ of the cathedral in Bern to show their scorn for the iconoclasts who had taken possession of the building. Hottinger[17] reports the incident as follows:

> Auch die Musik beym Gottesdienste ward abgeschafft. Am Abende des letzten Vincenzius-Festes [7 Feb., 1528] spielte der Organist die Tonweise des Liedes: "Ach armer Judas was hast du gethan?" und verliess dann mit Wehmuth die schöne Orgel, welche nun sogleich zerschlagen ward.

The followers of Luther satirized the Swabians in "Ain anders lied sagt von den schwaben, wy sie von gotts wort abgefallen sindt, im thon 'o du armer Judas,' " which is too long to reprint here.[18] The first of the eight stanzas runs:

> O ir armen Schwaben,
> was hand ir geton,

---

[15] Hildebrand (p. 59) cites Gropp, *Samml. würzb. Geschichtsschr.*, I, 130. I cannot find the passage in question in *Collectio Novissima Scriptorum et Rerum Wirceburgensium . . . P. Ignatii Gropp*, Frankfurt, 1741. See also *Anzeiger für Kunde der deutschen Vorzeit*, II (1854), 271.

[16] O. L. B. Wolff, *Sammlung historischer Volkslieder und Gedichte der Deutschen*, 1830, p. 258; Liliencron, *Die historischen Volkslieder*, III (1867), 480, No. 381.

[17] *Geschichte der Eidgenossen während der Zeiten der Kirchentrennung, Zweyte Abtheilung*, Zürich, 1829, pp. 117–118. See also E. E. Koch, *Geschichte des Kirchenliedes und Kirchengesanges der christlichen, insbesondere der deutschen evangelischen Kirche*, Stuttgart, 1867, II, 5; H. Alt, *Der christliche Cultus*, I (Berlin, 1851), 144; *Niklaus Manuel*, ed. J. Baechtold (*Bibliothek älterer Schriftwerke der deutschen Schweiz und ihres Grenzgebietes*, II, Frauenfeld, 1878), p. xxxv; Böckel, *Psychologie der Volksdichtung*, Leipzig, 1906, p. 331, n. 4. The story is poetically told in Carl von Winterfeld, *Der evangelische Kirchengesang*, I (Leipzig, 1843), 114–115.

[18] Bartsch, *Beiträge zur Quellenkunde der altdeutschen Literatur*, Strassburg, 1886, pp. 308–310, No. 3; K. Steiff, *Geschichtliche Lieder und Sprüche Württembergs*, 1899 ff., p. 336, No. 69.

"O Du Armer Judas"

> das wir unsern Christum
> so schandtlich hand verlon!
> darum so must ir liden
> dSpanier in euwerm land,
> des kaisers aigen bliben:
> ist euch ain grosse schand.

Perhaps the best stanza is the prophecy of the fate of the city of Ulm:

> Ullm, Ulm, ich thun dir sagen,
> es wirt dir ubell gan;
> denen mocht ir hertz schlagen,
> die by dir musen stan
> und hertzlich schmertzen liden,
> die grosse schmach und schand
> an iren kindt und wiben
> im gantzen Schwaben land.

The author discreetly conceals his identity:

> Der uns dis lied gesungen hatt,
> von nuwem hatt gemacht,
> der hatt der Spanier boshait
> von hertzen recht betracht,
> die sy iezund üben
> zu Ulm in der statt;
> darum well gott behüten
> ein lobliche eidgenossenschaft.

The presence of the Spanish in Swabia vexes this anonymous writer, but it so delights Jörg Lang of Simelbrunnen, an opponent of the Reformation, that he shouts "Kyrie, die Spanier seind im land!"—a stirring refrain to "Von den Reichstetten Ein newes Lied Im Thon 'Ach du armer Judas'" of 1546, which begins:

> We euch, ir armer reichstett,
> wie gross vermessenheit
> dass ir euch widern frommen kaiser,
> die höchste oberkait,
> on ursach dorften setzen
> auss besonderm neid und hass!
> furwar, ir solten wöllen,
> ir hettens betrachtet bass,
> Kyrie, die Spanier seind im land![19]

---

[19] Cf. Böhme, p. 646; Liliencron, *Die historischen Volkslieder*, IV (Leipzig, 1869), 369-372, No. 539; Hildebrand and Soltau, *Deutsche Historische Volkslieder, Zweites Hundert*, Leipzig, 1856, pp. 221-229, No. 30; Hildebrand, p. 64, n. 2; Hoffmann von Fallersleben, p. 232.

Taylor

The poet then in a leisurely manner goes about his task of calling the imperial cities to account. These cities, he says, have fallen away from the true faith because of their pride and particularly because of their acceptance of the Lutheran heresies:

> Wann ir aber thut fragen,
> was euch dahin hab bracht:
> furwar ich will euch sagen,
> ir habt euch zu hoch geacht
> und ewerer predicanten
> new falsch erdachte ler;
> wann ir sie alle hänkten,
> die thetens nimmer mer.
> Kyrie, die Spanier seind im land!

Next having reviewed the failure of the Peasants' War, in which the imperial cities participated, he admonishes them not to be angered at the judgment of God to be seen in its outcome:

> Furwar ir sölt nit zurnen,
> dann es kain wunder ist;
> wann gott der herr thut bschirmen,
> so hilft kain gwalt noch list.

The sins of the imperial cities, which are of course the sins of Luther's adherents, are numerous: nine stanzas are required to summarize them. The cities have refused obedience to their lord, the Emperor, have expelled priests, monks, and nuns, have sacked the churches and monasteries, have desecrated the holy images, mocked the mass, falsified Holy Writ, disregarded the times for fasting and have eaten meat on Friday, have scorned Charles V, their lawful ruler, and have rebelled against him. All this makes a very telling indictment of sins for which God's vengeance will not be long delayed:

> ob es sich schon lang hat verzogen;
> gott ist kain Bair nit,
> er hat noch niemand betrogen
> und kumbt zu rechter frist.
> Kyrie, die Spanier seind im land![20]

The concluding strophes in which he turns more to the personalities are distinctly weaker, and more than once degenerate into the vilest abuse.

---

[20] Stanza 13, vv. 5-9. Hildebrand and Soltau (*loc. cit.*) conjecture that the author of the satire was, in spite of these lines, a Bavarian.

"O Du Armer Judas"

Another employment of the Judas song is preserved in the manuscript of the unpublished chronicle of Thuringia and Erfurt by Konrad Stolle. The portion of the chronicle which can be certainly ascribed to Stolle closes with the year 1493 and up to that date the manuscript is in his autograph. There follow in various hands miscellaneous songs concerning events which took place in and after 1526, and among these songs occurs "Ein O Armer Judas von den newen Christen":

>O jr viel armen christen
>was hand jr getan,
>das jr euch Priapisten,
>hant so verfueren lan,
>darumb muest jr noch leiden
>vil hellische pein,
>sanct Peters schiffla meiden
>falt jn das mher hinein
>kyrieleison.
>
>Nit neyd die hohen schulen,
>wuthet nit mit schalle
>sie land nit also wulen.
>wie es euch gefal.
>wissen kein grund noch glauben,
>bey potencia,
>seint jr die selen brauben
>vnther falschem schein
>kyrieleyson.
>
>O jr reudigen scheffle,
>wer hat euch verblendt,
>das ir furwitzig effle,
>nit ewern hirten kendt,
>den wolffen thut nach lauffen,
>gand willig zu dem tod,
>got wirt euch schwerlich straffen,
>jr thuts an alle noth,
>kirieleyson.[21]

Nor did Luther himself fail to seize this weapon and turn it against his enemy, Duke Henry of Brunswick, saying, "Wenn

---

[21] Hesse, "Aus Konrad Stolles Erfurter Chronik," *Zeitschrift für deutsches Alterthum*, VIII (1851), 339–340 (Blatt 314 of the *Chronik*). Stolle remarks in another place that he was sixteen years old in 1446; it is therefore probable that the entries referring to the religious controversies and among them this song are by another.

ich dis Liedlin ein mal vol mache, wil ich dem zu Meintz seine leisen auch finden." The "Liedlin" is as follows:

>AH du arger Heintze, was hastu getan,
>Das du viel Fromer menschen durchs fewr hast morden lan.
>Des wirstu in der Helle leiden grosse pein,
>Lucibers geselle mustu ewig sein, Kyrieleison.
>
>AH verlorn Papisten, Was habt jr gethan,
>dass jr die rechten Christen, nicht kundtet leben lan,
>des habt die grosse schande, die ewig beliben sol,
>sie gehet durch alle Lande vnd solt ihr werden tol, Kyrieleison.[22]

Haltaus reports that at the instance of Duke Henry the Senate of Brunswick inquired in 1545 whether the gatekeepers of Wolfenbüttel had blown the tune "O du armer Judas" at the departure of the Senate's messengers, but he does not say whether a satisfactory answer was given.[23] Clearly the tune awakened far from pleasant recollections in the Duke's mind.

A mediocre song of 1548 aimed against Moritz of Saxony begins with the two foregoing stanzas of Luther's and continues:

>Moritz, du rechter Judas,
>was hastu gethan!
>du bringst zu uns die Spanier,
>die schenden fraw und man;
>du bringst her die Maraner
>in unser vaterland,
>darzu Italianer,
>ist dir ein ewig schand!

For a dozen and more strophes the satirist recites in a rather bitter tone the sins of Moritz and his associates. His wrath is perhaps expressed most forcefully in the last of the twenty-four stanzas:

>Sie söllen miteinander,
>die gotteslesterer all,

---

[22] *Wider Hans Worst* (1541), ed. J. K. F. Knaake, Halle, 1880, p. 73 (*Neudrucke deutscher Litteraturwerke des 16. und 17. Jahrhunderts*, No. 28). Cf. Hildebrand, p. 64; Liliencron, *Die historischen Volkslieder*, IV, 175, No. 476; Hassebrauk, "Die geschichtliche Volksdichtung Braunschweigs," *Zeitschrift des Harzvereins*, XXXIV (1910), 44. I have not seen Rambach, *Luthers Verdienst*, pp. 113–114.

[23] C. G. Haltaus, *Glossarium Germanicum Medii Aevi*, Leipzig, 1758, s.v. Judasgruss; he quotes from the *Acta Heinrici Iulii Ducis Brunsu. contra Ciuitatem Brunsu.*, I, 466. Cf. Creizenach, *Beiträge*, II, 186, n. 4.

"O Du Armer Judas"

> mit bapst und sein vasallen
> hinfahren ins teufels stall;
> daselbst sie sollen haben
> das ewige herzenleid.
> Herr gott, erschein mit gnaden
> deiner armen christenheit.[24]

In 1552 after the raising of the siege of Frankfurt the followers of Margrave Albrecht very savagely attacked Moritz for his treachery in a song to the tune of the *Judaslied:*

> O du armer Mauritz,
> was hastu gethan,
> das du den edlen kunig
> so schendlich hast verlan!
> darumb mustu leiden
> ewig spott und schand,
> man wirt dich zuletz vertreiben
> von leuten und von land,
> kistel seckel feger.

The remaining stanzas, three in number, heap up abusive and filthy epithets, displaying bitterness of feeling but no skill in expression. The second stanza will give an idea of the others:

> Wie oft bistu worden
> zu einem schelmen gross,
> getreten in Judas orden,
> verrathen viel ohn mass!
> kein trau noch ehr betrachtet,
> wider alle natur
> verretherei du machtest
> bist ie ein grosser laur,
> kisten seckel feger.[25]

When, a little later, Jacob Herbrot, burgomaster of Augsburg, took sides with Moritz of Saxony against the Emperor, the city was soon occupied by Spanish troops. The citizens relieved their feelings by singing:

> O du arger Herbrot,
> was hast dich angemast,
> dass du die stat Augspurg
> so grob verraten hast!
> darumb must du leiden
> und must billich sein
> dürrer bruder geselle
> an dem galgen sein.

---

[24] Liliencron, *Die historischen Volkslieder*, IV, 464–466, No. 572.

[25] *Ibid.*, IV, 568–569, No. 607. The last line, a parody of the Kyrie eleison, is also found in an Anabaptist mocking song based on the *Judaslied*, cf. Wackernagel, III, 392–393, No. 466.

Taylor

Each of the five stanzas begins in similar fashion: "O du loser Herbrot," "O du schneder Herbrot," and so on.[26] And the last one takes up the concluding "Lucifers geselle mustu ewig sein" so that in structure these satirical verses conform more nearly to their model than is the case with the other parodies.

A generation after this Gebhard Truchsess of Cologne was satirized to the tune of "O du armer Judas" (1587).[27]

The song was not forgotten by Roman Catholic partisans in the Thirty Years' War, but they seem to have employed it only against the "Winter King," Friedrich V. von der Pfalz, the unfortunate ruler of Bohemia; but Protestants, so far as the evidence now goes, made no use of it.[28] In 1620 a parody, which loses its force because of its length, thus threatened the Bohemians:

> O Ihr arme Böheim,
> was habt jhr gethon,
> das jhr ewern frommen König
> nit handt regieren lohn?
> Darumb müssent jhr euch leyden
> im gantzen Teutschn Landt,
> dess Kaysers gunst vermeiden,
> ist es nit ein schandt?
> Kyrie, thuns nimmer mehr.[29]

They have been false to their coronation oath and the emperor will not forgive their perjury:

> Bey der Crönung handt jhr geschworen
> einen falschen Aydt,
> sehent, das jhr nit werden verlohren
> darzu in ewigkeit,
> welches ist geschehen
> in manchem schönen Land,
> darff ich sicher jehen,
> ist es nit ein schandt?
> Kyrie, thuns nimmer mehr. . . .

---

[26] Liliencron, IV, 575–576, No. 609. Cf. his *Deutsches Leben im Volkslied um 1530*, p. LIV.

[27] Böhme, *Altdeutsches Liederbuch*, p. 647 (title only cited).

[28] K. Bruchmann, *Die auf den ersten Aufenthalt des Winterkönigs in Breslau bezüglichen Flugschriften*, Programm, Breslau, 1905, No. 215, contains nothing relevant here.

[29] R. Wolkan, *Deutsche Lieder auf den Winterkönig* (*Bibliothek deutscher Schriftsteller aus Böhmen*, VIII), Prague, 1898, pp. 82–86, No. 15, 2, cf. pp. 345–346, No. 68. Hildebrand (p. 64, n. 3) cites Heyse, *Bücherschatz der deutschen National-Litteratur des 16. und 17. Jahrhunderts*, No. 1338.

"O Du Armer Judas"

>Mein Gnädiger Herr, der Kayser,
>hat jhm gar recht gethan,
>das er sich in andere Landtschafft
>hat führen lohn.
>Da ist er euch gesessen
>mit Kraut und Loth,
>vnd wird ewer nit vergessen,
>vnnd solt es sein ewer Todt.
>>Kyrie, thuns nimmer mehr.

They deserve, the author continues, just such mockery as this song:

>Last euch nit verdriessen
>dieses Liedlin schlecht,
>man solt euch tretten mit füssen,
>so gescheh euch eben recht.

The bitterest scorn is heaped upon them:

>Nach disem Leben,
>jhr arme Böhmerleuth,
>Vngarer vnnd Mehrer
>vnd alles Dorngesteyd,
>was in den Hecken
>gewachsen ist im Landt,
>stellt man zu den Böcken
>am Jüngsten tag zur schandt.
>>Kyrie, thuns nimmer mehr.

All of them who revolt against their lawful lord, the Holy Roman Emperor, should, he concludes, be hanged like Absalom:

>Zur Schandt vnd Spot
>allem disem Gesindt,
>die wider den Römischen Kayser
>also vnrüwig seindt,
>denen wirdts ergohn,
>wie dem Absolon,
>an Baum ist er bliben hangen,
>mit Spiessen durchstechen lohn.
>>Kyrie, thuns nimmer mehr.

Another song to the tune of "O du armer Judas" appeared when the fall of the Winter King became certain: "Ein schön new Gesang Von König Fritzen" (1621).[30] The first stanza runs:

---

[30] Wolkan, pp. 117–123, No. 23; cf. p. 343, No. 60A; p. 363, No. 116; p. 384, No. 169E. This is presumably the song "O du armer Fritz," cited by Böhme, *Altdeutsches Liederbuch*, p. 647. See also K. Heyse, *Bücherschatz*, No. 1341 and Emil Weller, *Lieder des Dreissigjährigen Krieges*,² Basel, 1858, p. xxiii.

Taylor

> O du armer König Fritz,
> Was hast du gethan,
> Das du vnserem Keyser
> Seyn Cron hast nit gelahn?
> Darumb must du meiden
> Dein Chur vnd Böhmerland,
> Pfuy dich der grossen Schande,
> Ist aller Welt bekant.
>   Kyrie eleyson.

King Friedrich is addressed very directly at first:

> Ey lieber Fritz, mein lieber Gsell,
> Lass fahren dise Cron,
> Bereit ist dir woll in der Höll
> Für dich zu deinem lohn.
> Dan wer sich selbst erhöchen thut,
> Gott strafft in darauff glich,
> Falt tieffer in die helle Glut
> Vnnd kompt von Gottes Rych.
>   Kyrie eleyson.

The king's youth affords an opportunity for a home-thrust:

> O lieber Fritz, du junges Blut,
> Dir besser wer zu handt
> Ein gute eingeweichte Rut,
> Als dise grosse schandt.

His fall from high office is certain:

> Kein Chur Fürst wirst du nit mehr sein,
> Das sag ich dir fürwahr,
> Fileicht must hüten noch den schwein
> Auf dises künfftig jahr.
> Vertriben wirst auss Böhmerland.
> Sich was hast du gethan.
> An's Zepters statt in deiner handt
> Den narren kolben han.
>   Kyrie eleyson.

After this the author turns more to generalities: the Winter King's plans have gone awry because he was not called to office by the divine will. He would have been much better off as Elector than he is now in a position where the Catholics are watching him from every side. The soldiers of the Catholic "Liga" are well paid and in good spirits. The king has stolen from the

"O Du Armer Judas"

priests and they are now in arms. In short, the Winter King must soon pay the piper:

> Die Zech must jnen zahlen bar,
> Botz Fritz, du armer tropff,
> Beschichts nit hür, vffs ander jahr
> Fileicht mit deinem Kopff.
> Ich raht dier, flüch in Engelland
> In gute Sicherheit,
> Dein Pfaltz ist jetzt in ander hand,
> Mit trewen seis dir gseidt.
> Kyrie eleyson.

Here, if not earlier, the author might well have stopped, but he goes on for seven more stanzas. Friedrich has already suffered one defeat and he may look forward to the fate of Absalom:

> Sein vatter fromb wolt Absalon
> Vom Reich verstossen gar,
> Empfangen hat seinen lohn,
> Erhenckt sich an seim har.
> Das ebenbild dich treffen mag,
> Glaub Liechtenbergers Saag,
> Bestattet wirst in Esels graab,
> Vollenden deine tag.

Repentance will not save the Winter King from mockery and the consequences of his deeds. The author ends:

> Die sach wil ich jetzt bleiben lahn,
> Wo man nit folgen wil,
> Man sicht wol, wo es auss wil gahn
> Vnnd geben für ein Spil.
> Wer stercker ist, hat oberhandt,
> Ohn Gottes gnad ist nicht,
> Bewahre Catholischen Standt,
> Derselb behalt den stich.
> Kyrie eleyson.

This song is particularly interesting because it also occurs in a somewhat shorter form—sixteen stanzas instead of eighteen—with considerable verbal differences, called "Lamentatio über den König in Böhmen, von den Papisten gemacht."[31] For

---

[31] Opel and Cohn, *Der dreissigjährige Krieg, eine Sammlung von historischen Gedichten und Prosadarstellungen*, Halle, 1862, pp. 61–64; reprinted in Ditfurth, *Die historisch-politischen Volkslieder des dreissigjährigen Kriegs* (ed. K. Bartsch), Heidelberg, 1882, p. 18.

Taylor

comparison I print two corresponding stanzas[32] in parallel columns:

Die Pfaffen hast in harnisch bracht,	Die Pfaffen hastu in Harnisch bracht,
nit bald bringst sy mehr drauss,	Nicht mehr bringst du sie 'raus,
Bis dass sy dir den garaus gmacht	Bis sie dir han den Garaus gemacht
Vnd lachen dich nur auss,	Und kommst in nobis Haus.[33]
Den spot must sampt den schaden han	Den armen Judas musst du singen[34]
Mit deiner falscher Lehr,	Gar bald, mein lieber Friez,
Du hast es dir nur selbst gethan,	Vielleicht gar über die Klinge springen,
Ein ander mahl kommt mehr.	Dich wird brennen die Hiez.

To be sure the comparison of these two stanzas alone will not give an entirely fair idea of the degree of similarity existing between the two versions. Perhaps two-thirds of the stanzas agree as closely as the two foregoing, but the remaining third in "Ein schön new Gesang" have no correspondences in the "Lamentatio." Opel and Cohn, like all editors, think their version the more original, and possibly they are right. At any rate the characteristic idioms of the "Lamentatio" in the preceding passage appear as commonplaces in the parallel text, and this fact might be adduced in favor of their opinion.[35] The concluding stanza of the "Lamentatio"—which may be compared with that of the "Gesang" above—shows more than one humorous touch:

> Ich will der Sachen nicht thun zu viel,
> Wills itzund bleiben lan,
> Weil man kann sehen aus dem Brill,
> Was der Friez hat gethan.
> Wäre Bier in Fass widerum,

---

[32] On the left the tenth strophe of "Ein schön new Gesang" and on the right the eleventh of the "Lamentatio."

[33] "In nobis Haus kommen" means 'to die,' see Liebrecht, *Germania*, VII (1862), 500; and XVI (1871), 213; Laistner, *ibid.*, XXVI (1881), 65 ff.; Grimm, *Deutsche Mythologie*,[4] II, 837; J. Frey, *Gartengesellschaft* (ed. Bolte), Tübingen 1896, pp. 231–232; *Zeits. d. Vers. f. Volkskunde*, IV (1894), 189; J. W. Müller, *Album-Kern*, pp. 257–262 (cited in *Jahresberichte . . . germ. Philol.*, XXV [1903], 194, §12, No. 55); and a long series of notes in *Alemannia*, II (1875), 259–261; III (1875), 282; VII (1879), 94; IX (1881), 88; XIV (1886), 40 and in *Am Urquell*, I, 163 ff.; II, 34 ff., 112, 219, 260 ff. The phrase is of considerable interest to the mythologist.

[34] On "den armen Judas singen" see note below.

[35] Wolkan holds two contradictory opinions about the relation of the "Gesang" to the "Lamentatio"; compare p. vii with p. 343 and see Diemar in *Literaturblatt f. germ. und rom. Philol.*, XXI(1900), 163.

"O Du Armer Judas"

So stünde die Sache gar uol;
Zu geschehen Dingen in der Summ
Das Beste man reden soll.

The *Judaslied* is still sung by the Germans of western Bohemia[36] in the following form:

Ach falscher Judas, was hast du getan? Du hast ja unsern Herrn Gott verraten, jetzt musst du leiden in der Hölle Pein! Luci, Luciferi, es muss geschehen sein! Kyrieeleyson, Christeeleyson, Alleluja.
Wea[r] keina Oia [Eier] haut, Geld nehma a!

The last sentence, a request for the singer's pay, is of course not a part of the song; it refers to a custom which is practised in many places in Bohemia on Easter Monday: boys go from house to house singing and collecting eggs or other gifts which they later share among themselves.[37] The Judas song is, as will appear later in the discussion of its tune, intimately connected with Easter festivities. This instance of its being sung about Easter time by crowds of boys—presumably accompanied with more or less disorder—renders it probable that certain passages (collected by Creizenach) describing customs in olden times also refer to the *Judaslied*. On the Saturday before Easter, says Haltaus in a glossary of the German language written in 1758, the children of Leipzig used to go about with drums, bells, and rattles, singing a song in which Judas was mocked—presumably the Judas song:

Sonnabends vor Ostern, so bald es nur anfieng zu tagen, liefen die Kinder, Iungen und Mägdlein, mit Paucken, Schellen und Klappern durch die Stadt herumb, auch in die Klöster und Kirchen, und sungen mit grossem Geschrey ein teutsches lied, welches dem verraeter Iuda zuschand und unehren, von der geistlichkeit war gemacht worden.[38]

And a chronicler of Zwickau, a town of Saxony on the border of Bohemia, who is also quoted by Haltaus, gives a similar descrip-

---

[36] At "Kolosup bei Tuschkau, Mieser Bezirk"; see A. John, *Sitte, Brauch und Volksglaube im deutschen Westböhmen* (*Beiträge zur deutsch-böhmischen Volkskunde*, VI), Prague, 1905, p. 64.

[37] John, p. 67. See C. Peabody, "Certain Quests and Doles," *Putnam Anniversary Volume*, 1909, pp. 344-367 on this custom in general and the references in Sartori, *Sitte und Brauch*, III, 4.

[38] S.v. *Judasgruss*. He is quoting "Vogelius in Chron. Lips. MS."

Taylor

tion[39] of the "Pumpervesper" which was held there on Holy Thursday:

> Da iederman mit Stecken, Knütteln, Prügeln, Steinen, Hämmern, Beilen—in der Kirchen auf die Stüle und Bänke, und wo es nur einen starken Wiederhall gab, schlug. Darbey muste sich der arme Judas viel leiden; iederman redete alles übel von ihm und wolten ihn also zum Teufel in die Hölle jagen.

This shows certain reminiscences of phrases in "O du armer Judas." Jörg Wickram, an Alsatian of the sixteenth century, also refers unmistakably to the *Judaslied* in a collection of anecdotes entitled *Rollwagenbüchlein* (first ed., 1555). During Holy Week, he says, we tend to become pious, but when Easter passes, then the piety vanishes:

> Dann so jagen wir den Judas über den zaun vnd gan alle Kirchweyhen an; so muss sich Zacheus leiden gleich wie Judas in der finstern metten; mit dem und über den schreigt, singt und boldert man; wenig aber wirt dass leiden Christi bedacht.[40]

It is worth noting that in Bohemia something like the German *Judaslied* was sung in Holy Week, as the congregation left the church:

Jidáši co's ucinil	Oh Judas! What have you done?
ze's pana Krista Zidům zradil?	You have betrayed Christ to the Jews?
Musíš za to u pecle buti,	For this you shall live in Hell
S certem d'ablem prebyvati.	With the Devil as dues.

There is another Bohemian song about Judas which resembles the German song even more closely:

O Jidáši neverný!	O Judas, unfaithful one!
co jsi ucinil,	What have you done
ze's svého mistra	That you your Master
zidům prozradil?	Thus have betrayed?
musíš za to	For this you must
šlapat bláto,	Tramp in the mud
co nejvíce	As much as you can,
do cepice.	In depth to your cap.
My Jidáše honíme,	We are chasing Judas
klekáni zvoníme;	With kneeling and ringing of bells.
kyrie eyleson.[41]	

---

[39] Cf. Grimm, *Deutsches Wörterbuch*, VII, 1993 (Polterpassion), 2231 (Pumpermette, etc.), and VIII, 1488 (Rumpelmette), etc.

[40] Ed. H. Kurz, Leipzig, 1865, p. 88. "In der finstern metten" alludes to the mass read on Good Friday; the melody of the *Judaslied* in one early manuscript bears the superscription "Zu dem 'Laus tibi Christe' in der vinster metten."

[41] Both songs are carelessly printed by Solovev (pp. 116–117) from K. J. Erben, *Prostonárodní české písně a říkadla*, Prague, 1864, I, 60.

"O Du Armer Judas"

The melody of the *Judaslied* has a history of its own.[42] It is composed in the Mixolydian Mode, the seventh of the ecclesiastical modes, transposed a fourth higher. It is simple, direct and rather impressive.

This first appears, with minor differences, about the end of the fourteenth century (in a manuscript which can be dated between 1392 and 1400) under the title "Zu dem 'Laus tibi Christe,' in der vinster metten."[43] A Tegernsee manuscript of the next generation, which contains the melody, also refers

---

[42] F. M. Böhme, *Altdeutsches Liederbuch*, Leipzig, 1877, pp. 644 ff., No. 539; Liliencron, *Die historischen Volkslieder*, IV, Appendix, "Die Töne," pp. 24-25; Hoffmann von Fallersleben, pp. 230-232. Wilhelm Tappert (*Wandernde Melodien*,[2] Leipzig, 1890, pp. 80-81) adds nothing of importance. Böhme (p. LXVII), Liliencron (*Deutsches Leben im Volkslied um 1530*, pp. 227-228, No. 75), and Erk-Böhme (*Deutscher Liederhort*, III [Leipzig, 1894], 670, No. 1963) give transpositions into modern musical notation. There is another modern setting in a higher key in Friedrich Arnold, *Das deutsche Volkslied*, Prenzlau, 1912, II, 207, No. 139, cf. Anhang, p. 40; Arnold also has it composed in four part harmony.

[43] The melody in modern form is given in Erk-Böhme, III, 671, No. 1964, from whence the above is taken.

Taylor

to the employment of the tune in the services of the Church on Good Friday. The German text of the song runs:

> Eya der grossen liebe,
> die dich gebunden hat,
> gar hertiglich eim diebe,
> warer mensch und warer got.
> du hast her gegeben
> mit deinem blute rot
> uns das ewig leben,
> dank sey dir milter got.[44]

The last strophe of this hymn is the *Judaslied*. During the sixteenth century the tune was used for a hymn beginning:

> Wir dancken dir, lieber herre,
> der bitern marter dein . . . [45]

And of this again "O du armer Judas" is the last strophe. This combination of the Judas song with a hymn is, as Böhme (p. 646) points out, paralleled in several other instances, e.g., "O du armer Judas" is the last strophe of "Lob wollen wir singen."[46] He repeats Hoffmann von Fallersleben's conjecture that the "Laus tibi Christe" came originally from an Easter play in which the congregation sang the song in the vernacular; and the last strophe, "O tu miser Juda," is, he says, assigned to the congregation in printed texts of Easter plays from the sixteenth century. This fact alone would account satisfactorily for the people's familiarity with the melody. Easter plays which mention the Judas song are, however, rare. The stage directions in a Frankfort passion play[47] seem to confirm his surmise; at the moment when Judas kisses Christ the choir (*persone*) sings "O Juda quid dereliquisti." It should be remarked that the words as well as the melody can be traced back several centuries behind this; consequently it is unneces-

---

[44] P. Wackernagel, *Das deutsche Kirchenlied*, II (Leipzig, 1867), 467–468, No. 615 (from a manuscript of the first half of the fifteenth century, cf. Wackernagel, I, 365).

[45] Böhme, p. 645, No. 539; Wackernagel, II, 470–471, No. 623; *ibid.*, III, 392-393, No. 466; E. E. Koch, *Geschichte des Kirchenliedes*, I (Stuttgart, 1866), 209.

[46] Wackernagel, II, 472, No. 627. Cf. Heinrich Alt, *Der christliche Cultus*, II (Berlin, 1860), 494.

[47] Froning, *Das Drama des Mittelalters*, II, 355 (*Deutsche National-Litteratur*, XIV, 2). W. Tappert (*Wandernde Melodien*,² Leipzig, 1890, p. 80) says the song was sung in the Easter play when Judas leaves the stage to hang himself; but he does not cite any text in which this is done.

"O Du Armer Judas"

sary to insist on the importance of any Easter play in the dissemination of the Judas song.

The first appearance of "O du armer Judas" in print was, I think, in *Fünff und sechzig teutsche Lieder*, which is supposed to have been published in Strassburg between 1520 and 1525.[48] During the century of the Reformation the melody is found again and again in hymns: "Unser grosse Sünde" (1544), "Lob und Dank wir sagen" (1555).[49] But "Ein neuer armer Judas, dass über uns zu klagen ist, im alten Thone" (1527), an ecclesiastical parody of the *Judaslied*, seems not to have gained much popularity. Erk and Böhme give the first stanza:

> Ach wir armen menschen, was hab wir gethan
> Christum unsern Herrn gar oft verkauffet han!
> Müsst wir in der Helle leiden grosse Pein,
> wollte er selbst nicht Helfer und Mittler sein.[50]

Hermann Bonnus (d. 1548), a chronicler of Lübeck, adapted a Catholic hymn to this Protestant tune: "Och wy armen sünders" (1543). And before long this was translated from Low German into High German as "O wir armen Sünder," which may still be found in Evangelical hymn-books, both English and German.[51]

Thus one can say that this song about Judas has come down to the present day, for its melody may yet be heard; but the remark is only partly true. Certainly the impetus to the

---

[48] A. F. W. Fischer, Kirchenlieder-Lexikon, II, 220.

[49] Böhme (p. 646) lists some ten in all; see also Liliencron, *Deutsches Leben im Volkslied um 1530*, p. lii. Compare the list of adaptations and parodies given in W. Bäumker, *Das katholische deutsche Kirchenlied in seinen Singweisen*, I (Freiburg i. Br., 1886), 462–463, which adds some titles, e.g., "Der arge pyschof Annas"; "Pylatus hat gros vnreght."

[50] *Deutscher Liederhort*, III, 671.

[51] See for an elaborate account of the history of this hymn: A. F. W. Fischer, *Kirchenlieder-Lexikon*, Gotha, 1886, II, 219–220; cf. also Wackernagel, III, 735–736, Nos. 849, 850; Böhme, p. 646; and (for English translations) J. Julian, *A Dictionary of Hymnology*, rev. ed., London, 1907, p. 163. I have not seen H. Spiegel, *Hermann Bonnus*,[2] Göttingen, 1892 nor J. Zahn, *Die Melodien der deutschen evangelischen Kirchenlieder* (cited *Jahresberichte . . . germ. Philol.*, XV [1893], 234, §15, No. 76) nor Joseph Kehrein, *Kirchenlieder*, 1883, p. 153. Wendebourg (*Liederleben der evangelischen Kirche*, Hannover, 1852, p. 114, No. 45 and pp. 643–644) says that it is not assigned to Bonnus in the early hymnals and he therefore queries the ascription which is otherwise generally accepted.

Taylor

composition of "Och wy armen sünders" and its early popularity, evinced by its translation into High German, are due to the song. But the hymn has outlived its progenitor. Political songs to the same air no longer awaken the passions of men or their laughter and have now only an antiquarian interest. The verbosity of these satires, the narrowness of their outlook on the situation, and the vindictive, offensively personal feeling embodied in them destroy their effectiveness for us. Indeed the satires of the Reformation seem to have been almost, if not entirely, forgotten a hundred years later. The Protestants apparently did not think of the Judas song at all, although they had once been the first to employ it, and the Catholics used it only in one episode of the Thirty Years' War against one individual, the Winter King. Thus within a century the song had lost greatly in popularity and since then it has dropped entirely from view. But the root from which the satirical song and the Protestant (and Catholic) hymns sprang is alive in Bohemia where the song is still to be heard, as it was six centuries ago, at Eastertime.

ARCHER TAYLOR

Washington University

NOTE: "DEN ARMEN JUDAS SINGEN"

During the period of the greatest popularity of the Judas song as a model for satires the phrase "den armen Judas singen" was occasionally used. One instance has already been pointed out above in the "Lamentatio über den König in Böhmen." It means there as elsewhere "to sing rather small."[52] The phrase is employed in the Hegebacher *Chronik* in describing the attack of Georg Truchsess on the peasants during the Peasants' War; the chronicler says: "gleich an der gueten mitwochen [Osterwoche] wardent in "der arme Judas.'" With

[52] See J. and W. Grimm, *Deutsches Wörterbuch*, IV, ii, 2351, s. v. *Judas*. Long ago this meaning was remarked by Scherzius (*Glossarium Medii Aevi*, col. 745) when he defined *Judasgruss* as follows: "acclamatio infamis rhythmica Judae, in ludis scenicis olim decantata . . . sic cantilena similis a populo infamatis occini solita. dicebatur der arme Judas ab exordio. hunc & einem den armen Judas nachblasen." Scherzius cites as authority Haltaus, *Glossarium Germanicum Medii Aevi*, Lips., 1758.

Note: "Den Armen Judas Singen"

a similar connotation the phrase appears twice in the *Faustbuch* of 1587:

Es ist hie zu sehen des Gottlosen Fausti Hertz und Opinion, da der Teuffel jhm, wie man sagt, den armen Judas sang, wie er in der Hell seyn muste.[53]

and:

Als nu der Geist Fausto den armen Judas genugsam gesungen, ist er wiederum verschwunden, und den Faustum allein gantz Melancholisch und verwirrt gelassen.[54]

In view of these instances there is no reason for believing (with Hildebrand, p. 65) that the phrase implied that Judas himself sang the song in a play—the possibility that the Judas song came originally from an Easter play is another matter, which has already been discussed. It will be observed that the phrase "den armen Judas singen" was used only during the epoch when the Judas song was current and that it died with the disappearance of the satirical songs.

[53] Ed. W. Braune, Halle, 1878, p. 17, ch. iii at end (*Neudrucke deutscher Litteraturwerke des 16. und 17. Jahrhunderts*, Nos. 7–8b); ed. Scheible, *Das Kloster*, II, Stuttgart and Leipzig, 1846, p. 947.

[54] Ed. Braune, p. 113, ch. lxv at end; ed. Scheible, p. 1061.

Washington University Studies

Vol. VIII　　　　OCTOBER, 1920　　　　No. 1

JUDAS ISCARIOT IN CHARMS AND INCANTATIONS

ARCHER TAYLOR
Assistant Professor of German

Among the manifold uses to which the name and fame of Judas Iscariot were put in the traditional lore of the Middle Ages — and the Arch-Traitor as pattern of all evil in the accepted *Vita*, as example of God's merciful justice in the Brandan narrative, as accessory embellishment of wickedness in sundry tales and legends, has played many variegated rôles — not the least surprising, surely, is that in a charm for Christians to conjure with. Although this employment of Judas' name was of course frowned upon by Holy Church, still, notwithstanding that hostility (which explains the comparative scantiness of the material), there are sufficient examples to justify a brief discussion. These Judas incantations, which have in common with the old Germanic spells only the notion that one's end could be attained by conjuring with a comparison between two things, are interesting to a certain extent as illustrations of the usual Christian charm, which draws a parallel between the result desired and an event in Biblical history or tradition.[1] Some of them are curious because of the obscurity of the tradition they allude to. Noteworthy also, as showing the tenacity of folk-tradition, is the fact that, in spite of the express condemnation by the Church

---

[1] See, e.g., Ebermann, *Blut- und Wundsegen in ihrer Entwicklung dargestellt* (*Palaestra*, XXIV), Berlin, 1903; or Verdam, "Over bezweringsformulieren," *Mededeelingen van de Maatschappij der nederlandsche Letterkunde te Leiden over*

in the seventeenth century, the same Judas charms are current today in France. The following paragraphs aim to include whatever of value can be ascertained at present. I begin with the modern examples.

The name of Judas in charms is, I believe, always employed in connexion with some event in the life of Christ. Frequently there is a comparison — although its appositeness is not obvious in every instance — between the object to be attained and an incident of Judas' life as recorded in the Gospels. The most popular allusion is, as might perhaps have been expected, to the betrayal of the Savior or to the false kiss of the traitor. Thus the French peasants of l'Yonne say to the whirlwind:

> Esterbeau, esterbillon malin, je te conjure comme Judas conjurait Jésus-Christ le jour de Vendredi-Saint.[2]

Not far away a very similar conjuration is directed against the canker:

> Chancre blanc, chancre gris, chancre noir, telle sorte que ce soit, sors de la bouche de . . ., apaise ton feu comme Judas apaisa sa colère en trahissant Notre Seigneur Jésus-Christ au Jardin des Oliviers.[3]

From the Bourbonnais comes an analogous charm against the same ailment, but with a slight difference:

> Au nom du Père, du Fils, et du Saint-Esprit (*trois fois*). Chancre, chancre, chancre (*ici on doit indiquer sa nature*). Sors de cet endroit, sors du corps de. . . Chancre, perds ta chaleur, comme Judas perdit sa couleur, quand il vendit Notre-Seigneur. Au nom du Père, du Fils, et du Saint-Esprit; chancre, par le soleil et par la lune (*trois fois*), sors d'ici.[4]

From Baugé, a town a little to the east of Angers and, like the localities in which the previous charms were collected, also in the northern third of France, there are reported four vari-

het jaar 1900-1901, Leiden, 1901, pp. 3-63. There is not, so far as I am aware, any collection of the charms mentioning Judas Iscariot.

[2] C. Moiset, "Les Usages de l'Yonne," *Bulletin de la société des sciences historiques et naturelles de l'Yonne*, Année 1888, p. 121. Sébillot (*Folklore de France*, I [Paris, 1904], 113, n. 1) reprints the charm with minor orthographical differences.

[3] F. Louis, "Prières populaires en Seine-et-Marne," *Revue des traditions populaires*, VII (1892), 243, No. 2.

[4] Pérot, "Prières, invocations, formules sacrées, incantations en Bourbonnais," *Revue des traditions populaires*, XVIII (1903), 298.

ants of this charm as a "conjuration spéciale des brûlures." These are as follows:

Place the patient on his knees, make the sign of the cross, and speak the following words in a low voice:

Feu, perds ta chaleur comme Judas perdit ses couleurs en trahissant N. S. Jésus-Christ dans le jardin des Oliviers!

Then make the sign of the cross again, saying:

(*First Variant*) Feu de Dieu, perds ta chaleur
   Comme Judas perdit ses couleurs
   Quand il vendit N.-S. Jésus-Christ
   Au Jardin des Olives!

(*Second Variant*) Feu de Dieu, perds ta chaleur comme Judas perdit ses couleurs au Jardin des Oliviers en trahissant Jésus-Christ!

Recite five paters and five aves.

(*Third Variant*) Pronounce mentally three times these words:

Brûlure, perds ta chaleur comme Jésus-Christ perdit ses couleurs dans le Jardin des Oliviers!

While one is reciting these words exhale softly in the form of the cross on the burn and gently trace a cross on it with the thumb, and then breathe thrice on the mark.

(*Fourth Variant*) Make the sign of the cross without uttering words or without employing the hand by inclining the eyes in the direction in which the hand is customarily moved and repeat mentally the words:

Brûlure, je te conjure au nom des trois principaux mystères:
   Le mystère de la Rédemption,
   Le mystère de l'Incarnation,
   Le mystère de la Sainte Trinité.

Brûlure, tu perdras ta chaleur et ton ardeur comme Judas a perdu ses couleurs au Jardin des Olives.

Follow this with the sign of the cross made mentally as before. Repeat three times.[5]

An example from north of Angers has been inaccessible to me.[6] As a cure for burns it is sufficient in the department of Loir-et-Cher, which is somewhat to the east of Angers, for a "wise woman" to repeat the following incantation. She need not visit the sick man, but must murmur the charm while inclining her head in his direction. The words are:

   O feu, cesse tes ardeurs,
   Comme Jésus perdit ses couleurs

---

[5] Fraysse, "Adjurations et conjurations au pays de Baugé," *Revue des traditions populaires*, XIX (1904), 489-490.

[6] *Revue de l'Avranchin*, II, 364 (cited by Sauvé, *Mélusine*, III [1886], col. 112).

> Au jardin des olives,
> Feu de Dieu, apaise ta chaleur.[7]

This instance is particularly curious because Judas has disappeared entirely from the spell and is replaced by his Master. The reason for the substitution is obvious: the descriptive phrase "perdit ses couleurs" was felt to be inappropriate when applied to the betrayer and seemed rather to fit the Saviour. On the origin of the phrase and its mutations I shall have more to say later.

Far to the east, in the department of Hautes Vosges, Sauvé asserts that practically the same charm is in general use as a cure for burns.[8] His version differs from the first of the Baugé variants only in reading "sa couleur" for "ses couleurs" and "trahit" for "vendit." He cites furthermore a version from Rupt-surMoselle in which the concluding phrases are rather more elaborated than in the spells already given, as follows:

> Quand il trahit Notre-Seigneur, Le jour de gran vendredi, à trois heures après midi. Au nom du Père, du Fils et du Saint-Esprit.

Moreover, the tradition of this charm can be followed to the extreme east of France and into Switzerland. Bonnet took it down in the Franche-Comté in this form:

> Feu (*en soufflant dessus*), perds ta chaleur
> Comme Judas perdit sa couleur
> En trahissant le saint Sauveur.[9]

Apparently quite unaware of the very respectable history and wide dissemination of the charm he remarks, "C'est idiot! Je n'en disconviens pas!" On the easternmost edge of France in the department of Ain adjoining Lake Geneva, this charm is said to lessen the burning of a wound and is recited after the following fashion:

---

[7] Houssay, "Coûtumes et superstitions de Loir-et-Cher," *Revue des traditions populaires*, XV (1900), 380.

[8] *Le Folk-Lore des Hautes Vosges*, Paris, 1889, p. 215 (reprinted from Sauvé, "Oraisons, conjurations et gardes des paysans vosgiens," *Mélusine*, III [1886], col. 112).

[9] "Superstitions médicales de la Franche-Comté," *Mélusine*, I (1877), col. 400.

> Feu de Dieu, perds ta chaleur, aussi vrai que Judas perdit ses couleurs quand il trahit Notre Seigneur Jésus-Christ notre Sauveur sur le Calvaire.[10]

Should this fail after it has been repeated three times, one should take recourse in Guillon's other charms for the same purpose, those which mention Jonah and the whale, and Daniel and the lions and omit Judas.

In Switzerland the incantation has been collected at least three times, once from Neuchâtel in a form resembling the expanded text current along the Moselle, but with the difference that it is now recommended for use in healing *tachet*, an eruptive, contagious ailment of the skins of men and animals. Elaborate directions are given, specifying how to gaze at the beast, how to pull its tail, and how to kiss its food (if it is eating), but these I omit:

> Feu chaud, feu froid, feu ardent, feu volant, feu brûlant, quel feu que ce puisse être, ainsi puisse-t-il perdre sa chaleur, sa force et sa vigeur, comme Judas perdit sa couleur le jour du Grand Vendredi Saint, à trois heures après midi. Au nom du Père, du Fils et du Saint Esprit. Amen.[11]

The charm seems to be in common use to the south of Lake Geneva (Haute-Gruyère) where it is thought, when repeated thrice, to benefit an inflammation in which gangrene is threatened. In this version, also, the phrase "perdit ses couleurs" caused the folk to hesitate with the result that the charm is much altered:

> Au nom du Père, etc. (Comme?) Judas était en fureur et en chaleur, par sa fureur et sa chaleur il changea de couleur, quand il trahit notre Seigneur. Au nom du Père, etc.[12]

Another charm, which is printed immediately after the foregoing, preserves the usual form:

> Feu, perds ta chaleur comme Judas changea de couleur quand il trahit notre Seigneur. Au nom, etc.

The northernmost locality in which these charms have been taken down is Liége in Belgium, where G. O. Hock cites two

---

[10] Guillon, "Prières populaires de l'Ain," *Revue des traditions populaires*, I (1886), 38.

[11] A. Piaget, "Prières et 'secrets'," *Musée Neuchatelois*, XXXIV (1897), 56.

[12] E. Lambelet, "Les croyances populaires du Pays d'Enhaut (Haute-Gruyère)," *Schweizerisches Archiv für Volkskunde*, XII (1908), 102, No. 28.

variant forms current about 1872.¹³ The shorter one is employed for burns, says the author's informant, when oil blessed in honor of St. Laurent is not available. The words seem to have undergone some corruption, for there is no clear parallelism between the two parts of the charm: "Brûlure! Arrête ta rigeur comme Judas a changé de visage!" The charm is also reported from the same region in the ordinary form:

Make the sign of the cross thrice over the burn and say:

Feu, perds ta chaleur comme Judas perdit sa couleur quand il trahit Jésus-Christ au jardin des Olives.

Then recite five paters and five aves in memory of the five wounds of our Saviour.

The dissemination of this charm has no doubt been very considerably aided by its inclusion in recipe-books for the lower classes, and this method of spreading and preserving it accounts for the rather monotonous uniformity of the variants. The changing fortunes and instable contents of one such book, entitled *Le Médecin des Pauvres*, are discussed (for the years after 1821, the date of the earliest existing copy) by Ebermann.¹⁴ The Judas charm appears to be one of the more permanent constituents of the booklet, being absent in but two out of fourteen copies. This significance of this fact can hardly be overrated, inasmuch as Ebermann calls the chapbook the "vademecum of the French employers of charms." Here the charm in its familiar guise is recommended for a burn (Ebermann, p. 139, I, 7) and again in combination with a different and equally well established formula (p. 143, II, 1):

Blow on the wound three times in the form of a cross and say to St. Laurent:

Sur un braisier ardent, — vous retourniez et n'étiez pas souffrant, — fraites-moi la grâce — que cette ardeur se passe, — feu de Dieu, perds ta chaleur — comme Judas perdit sa couleur, — quand pour sa passion juive, — il trahit Jésus au jardin des Olives, (*et après avoir nommé la personne vous ajouterez:*) Dieu t'a guéri par sa puissance.

Its use for the chancre, which is rather less frequent than in the

---

¹³ *Croyances et remèdes populaires au pays de Liége*, Liége, 1872, pp. 124 and 243, respectively. Ebermann's reference (*Zs. des Vereins f. Volkskunde*, XXIV [1914], 139) to p. 130 seems to be an error.

¹⁴ *Zs. des Vereins f. Volkskunde*, XXIV (1914), 134-62.

popular charms, is recommended once by the booklet (Ebermann, p. 152, VIII, 15):

<small>Chancre blanc, chancre rouge, chancre douloureux, éteins ton feu et ta rougeur comme Judas a perdu sa couleur quand il a trahi Notre Seigneur.</small>

In a late and greatly enlarged text of the *Médecin des Pauvres* a mutilated version is suggested for use in case of colic (Ebermann, p. 157, XIV, 34): "Colique passez, colique fâche, colique, va-t-en comme Judas a trahi Notre Seigneur au Jardin des Olives." And finally in the same corrupted text of the pamphlet the charm in a still different form is employed to stop lightning (Ebermann, p. 159, XIV, 71): One should take a Christmas egg and throw it toward the lightning, saying "Que Dieu t'arrête, comme Judas arrêta Jésus-Christ au Jardin des Oliviers."

All of these modern instances come from a comparatively restricted area, a belt lying north of the Loire and extending eastward from the Atlantic Coast into Switzerland and northward into Belgium, but the material as a whole is too scanty to permit any sound inference from this fact. In a great part of this region *chaleur* and *couleur* are pronounced alike, a peculiarity which distinguishes the local dialects from Parisian and Central French. The possibility of confusion which thus arises is perhaps to be seen at work in the phrase "comme Judas perdit sa couleur" (presumably originally *chaleur* to correspond with the other half of the formula, which would then be "Perds ta chaleur comme Judas perdit sa chaleur.") The effectiveness of a charm seems to be due to the exactness of the comparison; note for example in the first spell "je te conjure comme Judas conjurait." It is of some interest in tracing the migration of traditional lore to observe that this charm with the reading *couleur* has been translated into German:

<small>Feuer, feuer, feuer,
Verliere deine hitz,
Wie der Judas seine farb verloren hat,
Als er den herrn Jesus Christus verrathen hat.
Im namen u. s. w.[15]</small>

<small>[15] Wolf, "Segen," *Zeits. f. deutsches Altertum*, VII (1849), 536, No. 14.</small>

The use of just this sort of formula was condemned by Jean Baptiste Thiers, in his *Traité des Superstitions* (1st ed., Paris, 1679). He selects for reprehension the following charm for erysipelas: "Feu! je te conjure de perdre ta fureur, comme fit Judas devant notre Seigneur," and for a scald or burn: "Feu! perds ta chaleur comme Judas perdit sa couleur, lorsqu'il trahit notre Seigneur."[16] But beyond a blanket condemnation he does not go and the reason for his objecting to the use of these charms does not appear.

The traitorous kiss of Judas is mentioned in an obscure Greek charm reprinted by Rouse from a manuscript collection of medical lore more than a century old — a charm which "has apparently been copied from an older document, or written down from memory, and much blundered." Rouse translates it, so far as it is intelligible, as follows:

> Beyond Jordan stands a youth, the hateful Half-head; and cries with a loud voice that he wants man's flesh to eat. Then came a voice from heaven, which said [something or other in reference to King Pharaoh and the kiss of Judas, our Lord, the Virgin Mary, and Aaron, adding:] Depart and flee from the servant of God, N or M.[17]

A long charm against thieves, printed by Birlinger from a German manuscript of 1727, mentions both the betrayal and the false kiss of Judas:

> Ich beschwöre dich bey Maister Arbegast, der allen dieben ein Maister was, der sei bundten und knipft und nimmermer auffgelöst biss ahn jungsten tag. da soll dir so bandt sein als dem Judas wahr, da er unser lieber herr Jesus Christus verkaufft hat, so bandt sol dir sein dieb und diebin; wan du wült stehlen das mein, so solst du gefangen und gebunden sein; da solt so wenig ruoh haben als Judas hat, da er unserm lieben herrn Jesum Christum einen falschen kuss gab, so bang sol dir sein dieb . . . Du dieb oder diebin solt wenig weichen von meinem guot, biss dass du mir kannst zehlen die staudten, die über die erden ausluogen, du muost mir bei meinem guoth still stahn, biss unser liebe frau ein andren Sohn

---

[16] Quoted by F. Liebrecht, *Des Gervasius von Tilbury Otia Imperialia*, Hannover, 1856, p. 255 ("Französischer Aberglaube," Nos. 446 and 447) and by Solovev, *K legendam ob Iudye predatelye*, Kharkov, 1898, p. 194.

[17] "Folk-lore from the Southern Sporades," *Folk-lore*, X (1899), 171-172. On the mysterious "Half-head," which Rouse does not explain, see Abbott, *Macedonian Folk-lore*, p. 363 and F. Pradel, *Griechische Gebete aus Süditalien*, pp. 81, 93 (Religionsgeschichtliche Versuche und Vorarbeiten, III, 333, 345); the ancient ἡμικρανία, which is here personified, later became the French migraine.

JUDIAS ISCARIOT IN CHARMS AND INCANTATIONS 11

gebehrt und ich dich in des Teuffels namen urlaub geb im nahmen Gottes vatters und des Sohnes und des hl. Gaists. amen.[18]

This is a rather unusual form of a curse or charm which has a long history in German sources. A second incantation, also printed by Birlinger from the same manuscript, follows more closely the traditional type. It is much more cleverly constructed: the effect of disobeying the injunctions is compared to episodes of the betrayal and sale of Christ as reflected in Judas' mind, and the injunctions are accompanied by a blasphemous imitation of the Crucifixion. One is told to take three new horseshoe nails and drive them into a candle, saying:

Ir tieb und tiebin, ich gebite euch bei dem ersten nagel, den ich dir in dein hirn und stirn geschlagen: es sol dir so wint und weh werden nach dem menschen und nach dem ort, wo du es genummen hast, als dem jünger Judas war als er Christus verraten hat.

Ich gebiete dir bei dem andern nagel, dass ich dhir in dein lunken und leberen thuo schlagen: es sol dir so wint und weh werden nach dem menschen und nach dem orth, wo du es genumen hast, als dem jünger Judas war, als er die 30 pfennig wider bracht!

Ich gebiete und bint dich bei dem dritten nagel, den ich dir in dein herz und fiess thuo schlagen, auf dass- du das gestohlen wider an sein gehöriges ort bringest, wo du es genomen hast: es sol dir so wint und weh werden nach dem menschen und nach dem orth, wo du es genommen hast, als dem jünger Judas war, da er Christus verraten und verkauft hat!

Ich gebiet dir bei den heiligen 3 negel, die Christus durch sein heilige hent und fiess seint geschlagen worten; o tieb, ich beschwör dich und gebiet dir bei den hl. 3 negel, dass du das gestohlen guot widder bringen must; ich beschwör dich bei dem höchsten Got, der über alle creaturen gewalt ist, der ist genant her Jesus Christ, amen. Binte S. Peter bint! S. Peter sprach: ich hab schon gebunten, dass er das gestolen gut wider bringen anheim thuot, wo er es hat genommen Gott vater u. s. w.[19]

Weinhold reports that a similar, but somewhat corrupted version of the charm—with the added stipulation, peculiar to this instance, that the nails should have been made on a Friday—was employed in Upper Styria about 1812.[20] And a version which is practically identical with this last is printed by Dörler, who dates it about two generations later and local-

[18] "Volkstümliches aus der Baar [Baden]," *Alemannia*, II (1875), 128, No. 4.
[19] *Ibid.*, pp. 128-129, No. 5.
[20] "Ein Diebsegen," *Zs. des Vereins f. Volkskunde*, VIII (1898), 346.

izes it in the Tyrol. To regain stolen property, says Dörler, the owner should go before sunrise to a pear-tree, hold towards the east three nails from a bier or three new horseshoe nails, which have been annointed with the fat of a sinner, and say:

"O Dieb! ich binde dich bei dem ersten Nagel, den ich dir in deine Stirn und Hirn thu schlagen, dass du das gestohlene Gut wider an seinen vorigen Ort musst tragen; es soll dir so weh werden, nach dem Menschen und nach dem Ort, wo du es gestohlen hast, als dem Jünger Judas war, da er Jesum verrathen hatte. Den andren Nagel, den ich dir in deine Lung und Leber thu schlagen, dass du das gestohlene Gut wieder an seinen vorigen Ort musst tragen; es soll dir so weh nach dem Menschen und nach dem Ort sein, da du es gestohlen hast, als dem Pilato in der Höllenpein. Den dritten Nagel, den ich dir, Dieb, in deinen Fuss thu schlagen, dass du das gestohlene Gut wieder an seinen vorigen Ort musst tragen, wo du es gestohlen hast. O Dieb, ich binde dich und bringe dich durch die heiligen drei Nägel, die Christum durch seine heiligen Hände und Füsse sind geschlagen worden, dass du das gestohlene Gut wieder an seinen vorigen Ort musst tragen, wo du es gestohlen hast." [21]

This very same charm is reported from Westphalia about the middle of the last century.[22]

It is clear that such a long and complex charm, employing comparisons which do not in all probability occur readily to the popular mind, must have been handed down during the two centuries of its attested existence by manuscript recipe-books; the spoken word could only be of secondary importance in the transmission of such an incantation. Its antiquity, its wide dissemination, and the accuracy with which it is re-

[21] "Zaubersprüche und Sympathie-Mittel aus Tyrol," *Zs. für österreichische Volkskunde*, II (1896), 152.

[22] Kuhn, *Sagen, Gebräuche und Märchen aus Westfalen*, Leipzig, 1859, II, 194-195. See also the analogous charms there cited in which, however, Judas does not appear; cf. further Klapper, *Zs. f. deutsche Philologie*, XLVII (1916), 88-89; Rochholtz, "Aargauer Besegnungen," *Zs. f. deutsche Mythologie*, IV (1859), 130; Bolte and Polívka, *Anmerkungen zu den Kinder- und Hausmärchen*, III, 453; Mogk, *Germanistische Abhandlungen*, XII, 109-118; Kinder, *Am Urdsbrunnen*, VII, 170 ff.; *Am Urquell*, III, 136, 219 f., 235 f.; *Ethnologische Mitteilungen aus Ungarn*, II, 97 f.; McBryde, *Modern Language Notes*, XXII, 168 f.; *Mitteilungen des nordböhmischen Exkursionsklubs*, XVIII, 175, 259 f., XIX, 47 f., 170, 253 f.; Haas, *Blätter für pommersche Volkskunde*, IV, 119 f., 139, 141, 158, 169; Freund and Weineck as cited in *Jahresberichte über . . . germanische Philologie*, XIII (1891), 192, § 10, Nos. 328, 329; and the many references to such charms in Sartori, *Sitte und Brauch*, III, 18.

peated, notwithstanding its length and intricacy, all indicate this manner of transmission.

The ultimate suggestion for this long and involved charm is, I am inclined to think, the so-called Judas curse, the history of which I have traced elsewhere.[23] The curse expressed a hope that, if the deposer broke his oath, he might share the lot of Judas (*habeat partem cum Juda*). It was frequently used by the Church and people connected with the Church to add dignity to formal documents of gift, deeds, and the like. In particular it was very widely used in manuscripts as a threat intended to protect the books of a monastery. On this account and perhaps for other reasons, the curse came in the later Middle Ages to be associated with thieves. John Wier, who is one of the first and also one of the sanest writers on witchcraft, roundly condemns the use of the *anathema sancti Adalberti*, as he calls the Judas curse, to force the return of stolen property.[24] Frommand, the compiler of a learned treatise on magic, *De Fascinatione* (1675), calls the anathema "incantamentum magicum" (p. 708) and recites the theological objections to its use; but he may have got most of his information from Wier. The curse known to these writers is an elaborate construction in which the Trinity, the Virgin, and the saints are invoked against "illos fures, sacrilegos, seu raptores, operarios, consilarios, coadiutores, coadiutrices, qui hoc furtum siue malum perpetrauerunt, siue sibi inde aliquid usurpauerunt." They are damned with the fate of Dathan and Abiram, Judas and Pilate, et al., with all the ingenuity of

---

[23] See a forthcoming number of the *American Journal of Philology*.

[24] *De praestigiis daemonum*, Basel, 1583, col. 522-524, lib. V, c. vi, "Ut Res furto sublata restituatur, anathema magicum." He says: "Anathema hoc S. Adalberti magicum potius ob diuini nominis & sacrae Scripturae abusum, quam Christianum, hic ea adjicio ratione, ut occulta eiusmodi actionum plerisque religiosis hominibus usitarum impietas oculis omnium magis eluceat." Why the charm (curse) is associated with Saint Adalbert is not explained; possibly information on this score might be found in R. F. Kaindl, "Literatur zur geschichte des heiligen Adalbert," *Mitteilungen d. österr. inst.*, XIX-XX (cited from R. J. Kerner, *Slavic Europe*, No. 2660), but that volume of the periodical is inaccessible to me.

the mediæval mind. The employment of the curse against thieves, as here, was pretty certainly the starting-point for the preceding formulæ which have acquired more nearly the form of the orthodox charm; note especially the first incantation against thieves (*Ich beschwöre dich*, &c.) in which the underlying concept wavers back and forth between the curse and the charm. The development half complete may be seen in an anathema of the bishop of Czernowitz. In 1786 Dosothei, Bishop of the Imperial Bukovina, was informed by Theodor Halip, priest in the village of Oprisheni, that he (the priest) had suffered the loss of some of his cattle and that a fellow-villager had also complained of thefts. By virtue, accordingly, of the power entrusted to him the bishop issued a formal anathema against the thieves and their accomplices in the following terms:

That all of them should be cursed by God the Lord, the just Judge and Saviour, Jesus Christ, by His most pure Mother, by the twelve apostles, by the 318 fathers of the council at Nicæa, and by all saints. Iron, ore, and stone and all hard substances should decay, but their bodies should persist uninjured and undissolved after death! In eternity their souls should partake with Judas of eternal torments, but in this world the wrath of God should rest upon them and be poured over them and their children! They should have no success in life, their labors and efforts should accomplish their own destruction. . . The tremor of Cain and the sores of Gehazi should cling to their bodies. . . Those who know and disclose the evildoers shall be pardoned, and they shall be blessed by God, the Lord. So may it be.[25]

From such a curse as this it is no very long step to the formulæ given above.

Though the long spell which has just been discussed seems, according to the present conjecture, to have had its starting point in the Judas curse, other charms show developments in different directions which are not easily referable to the curse, and which, moreover, contain unfamiliar traditions.[26] It seems

[25] Kaindl, ''Beiträge zur Volkskunde Osteuropas,'' *Zs. des Vereins f. Volkskunde*, XXVII (1917), 240-241, No. 20, ''Fluchbrief gegen Diebe'' (quoted from F. A. Wickenhauser, *Geschichte des Bistums Radautz*, I, 191 ff.)

[26] The following charm, which occurs in a collection of recipes of the 16-17th century in Nuremberg, although it refers to Judas, does not apparently belong in the present collection:

> Longienus [sic] ein Judasritter was,
> der gott dem herrn seine heylige seitten durchstach,

reasonably clear that these originated independently. The incident alluded to in a North German charm for toothache I cannot identify; it may refer to some definite popular belief, or merely to the natural supposition that Christ would avoid Judas' house:

> Zahnweh, sage, fahre aus
> Und meide du mein Haus,
> Gleichwie Christus Judas Haus gemieden hat.[27]

Nor has the South German notion that the day on which Judas died is favorable for charming away warts an obvious origin.[28]

The incantation preserved in a Bamberg manuscript of the thirteenth century is perhaps the most curious of all those in which Judas is mentioned. It is as follows:

> Christ unte iudas spiliten mit spieza. do wart der heiligo Xrist wnd in sine siton. Do nam er den dumen unte uor duhta se uorna. So uerstant du bluod so se iordanis aha verstunt do der heiligo iohannes den heilanden crist in iro tovfta. daz dir zo bvza. Crist wart hi erden wnt. daz wart da ze himele chunt. izne blotete. noch ne svar. noch nechein eiter ne bar. taz was ein file gote stunte. heil sis tu wunte. In nomine Jesu Christi. Daz dir ze buze. Pat. nost. ter et addens ter. Ich besuere dich bi den heiligen funf wnten. heil sis tu wunde. per patrem et filium et spiritum sanctum fiat. Amen.[29]

It was long thought that some bit of heathen mythology was hidden in the allusion to the conflict between Christ and Judas, inasmuch as such a conflict is not reported by the New Testament and seems to be no part of western Christian tradition. Some believed that perhaps the Saviour and His betrayer were really creatures of pagan myth under altered names. The comparison with the famous episode of the death

> doraus flos wasser vnd blutt.
> durch desselbigen bluttes ehre.
> verstehe, blutt, nicht mehre.
> im namen u. s. w. — Bartsch, ''Zauber und Segen,'' *Zs. f. deutsche Mythologie*, III (1855), 327.

[27] Haase, ''Volksmedizin in der Grafschaft Ruppin und Umgegend,'' *Zs. des Vereins f. Volkskunde*, VIII (1898), 201.

[28] Rehsener, ''Aus Gossensass: Arbeit und Brauch in Haus, Feld, Wald und Alm,'' *ibid.*, IV (1894), 109, n. 2.

[29] The phonology of this charm suggests a date considerably earlier than the thirteenth century; note, for example, the preservation of the full vowels in the inflectional endings. The traces of rhyme imply that the charm was originally composed in rough verses, which cannot now be successfully reconstructed.

of Baldr is obvious.³⁰ Baldr, according to the Norse story, dies at the hands of Hodr, the blind god, who throws a sprig of mistletoe at him. Loki has maliciously selected the only plant by which Baldr is vulnerable. This identification of the incident in the charm, seductive as it may seem, is no longer tenable. Reuschel has suggested, and he is surely right, that the event alluded to is narrated in the Arabic *Evangelium Infantiae*,³¹ Chap. xxxv, which tells how Judas' mother took him when he was still a child to Mary's house to play with Jesus, and how even at that early age the wickedness of the traitor manifested itself in his striking the Saviour on the right side. The identification of this incident with that mentioned in the charm has been recently developed at some length by Jacoby,³² who seems not to have noticed Reuschel's remark. He explains that the allusion in the charm to the weapons (*spieza*) with which the children are playing is an anticipation of the spear with which Longinus pierced His side and shows in some detail that the other comparisons — with which we are not now concerned — can be paralleled in other early charms. The incantation is therefore wholly Christian in origin, whatever may be the antecedents of the *Evangelium Infantiae*. We need not inquire precisely how the incident made its way from the Arabic Gospel into the West; there were various inlets of Arabic culture into western Europe, and Jacoby has pointed out that two other incidents from the same gospel appeared in Europe long before its first publication (in 1697). He might have added that the author of the *Gloucester Legendary* (before 1290) betrays an acquaintance with that apocryphal document; and perhaps other instances could be adduced.³³

³⁰ The discussions of Koegel, Detter, and Ebermann, all of whom held this view, are concisely summarized by Jacoby in the article cited below. See also Golther, *Handbuch der germanischen Mythologie*, Leipzig, 1895, p. 383, n. 1.

³¹ *Zs. des Vereins für Volkskunde*, XIV (1904), 354. *Cf.* Tischendorf, *Evangelia apocrypha*, 1876, pp. 199 f.

³² "Der Bamberger Blutsegen," *Zs. für deutsches Altertum*, LIV (1913), 200-209.

³³ See in general G. Baist, "Arabische Beziehungen vor den Kreuzzügen,"

JUDIAS ISCARIOT IN CHARMS AND INCANTATIONS

Such then are the charms in which Judas Iscariot figures. They seem to be all of Christian manufacture. Some kinship with the ancient Germanic spells might have been expected, but there is nothing in common between these and the Judas charms except the principle of comparison, which is of course primitive. Only the French charms suggested by a comparison with Judas' heat (paleness, wrath) at the time of his betrayal of Christ appear to have obtained any currency among the folk. The long German incantation is pretty clearly a bookish affair, which originated in a learned atmosphere and was handed down not by word of mouth but by the almanac and the recipe-book. All the others seem almost to be special or occasional developments, which have been preserved more or less by accident. They are curious individually for one reason or another, and as a whole they form a small chapter in the history of the Christian charm.

Verhandlungen der germanistischen Sektion der 49. Versammlung deutscher Philologen zu Basel, pp. 127 ff.; Geiger, *Zs. für deutsche Philologie*, XL (1908), 99; Suchier, *Zs. für romanische Philologie*, VIII (1884), 522 ff.; *Romania*, XXXI (1902), 158 (citing *Studj di filologia romanza*, VIII [1899-1901], 173); etc.

II.—THE JUDAS CURSE.

A recent article in this Journal discusses a very formal type of oath, termed by the writer the Judas Iscariot curse.[1] This oath has, however, a very much wider distribution than is there indicated. It consists, in its briefest form, of the wish that the wrong-doer should share the lot of Judas ("habeat portionem cum Iuda"); but, according to the mood of the user, this simple form may be much expanded by allusion to the great sinners of the Bible from Cain to Ananias and Sapphira. Amplified in this fashion, the Judas Iscariot curse becomes a terrifying anathema which can still be increased in effectiveness by hints of what its violator may expect at the Day of Judgment. Yet one suspects that the mediaeval listener to the oath often gave a more attentive ear to the threat of a fine, which the breaking of the oath incurred, than to its appalling phrases. Other imprecations were certainly felt to be more powerful, whereas the Judas curse remained a "formula anathematis minoris."[2] This fact appears plainly in an old German Chronicle where the Judas curse is the first and least of a long list of penalties arranged climactically. I extract a passage from the chapter in question (which is itself a single sentence extending over one and a third columns folio):

... vnd also soliche uorhorunge gescheen was, so fant sich kuntlich in denselben bullen vnd processen, das derselbe Friderich von dem egenanten consilium dise nachgeschribenn pene anathematis, das man in deutsche sprache nennet *Judas fluch*, dornach in die pene des grossen bannes, in latin genant *sacrilege*, dornach in die pene der berawbunge

---

[1] H. Martin, "The Judas Iscariot Curse," *supra*, XXXVII (1916), 434-451. John Aubrey, the seventeenth-century gossip and antiquarian, was, so far as I know, the first to show any sign of curious interest in the Judas curse. One of his notes reads: "In the grants to the Church by the Saxon King you may see in the Monasticon Angl. many direfull imprecations, as let them that ... be thrown into the abyss, and let their portione be with Judas Iscariot, &c."—*Remains of Gentilisme and Judaisme*, 1686-1687, Folk-Lore Society, IV (1881), p. 128.

[2] J. G. Scherzius, *Glossarium Germanicum Medii Aevi*, Argentorati, 1781, s. v. *Judasfluch*.

THE JUDAS CURSE.

aller vnd iglicher lehunge, die er besizet vnd innen haltet, baide von der heiligen kirchen vnd von dem reiche, vnd ander gaistlich vnd werntlich, dornach. . . .[3]

Solemn, dignified, juristic, and almost always lacking in any suggestion of popular or casual employment, this Judas Iscariot curse is suitable, as Martin (p. 442) says, for use in " political pronouncements, pontifical decrees including decrees of gift, epitaphs, and in poetry." In the following notes I adopt for convenience his arrangement, adding, however, separate headings for its special uses against thieves and for the protection of books.[4]

1. *Political Uses.* During the eleventh century the Judas curse was on one occasion published as widely in France as it had once been in the Roman Empire where Justinian exacted it of his praetorian prefects (Martin, pp. 443-44), for it was contained in the Papal Bull of 1035 proclaiming the Peace of God according to which all men were commanded to lay down their arms in expectation of the second advent of Christ. After

---

[3] Io. Burchardius Menckenius, *Scriptores Rerum Germanicarum praecipue Saxonicarum,* Tomus I (Lipsiae, 1728), col. 1106 (Cap. XLVI of Hist. Imp. Sigismundi). This incident may also be referred to by Birlinger (*Alemannia,* XVI [1888], 63, s. v. *Judenflueoh*), but the quotation is too brief to be clear.

[4] A very curious oath, which may have been used in conversation, is mentioned in a seventeenth-century translation of a Jewish life of Christ, the *Toldoth Yeshua:* " Und alle Weisen der Völker wissen dies Geheimniss, aber sie leugnen es, aber sie fluchen und schelten den Judas Ischariota, und wenn sie Hader und Streit unter einander haben, sagen sie einer dem andern, es geschehe dir, wie Judas Ischariota dem Jesus gethan."—S. Krauss, *Das Leben Jesu nach jüdischen Quellen,* Berlin, 1902, p. 100. The secret here alluded to is the story telling how Christ flew in the air before Queen Helena in order to prove His divinity. Judas rose into the air after Him and overcame his Master by an obscene trick. This episode is regularly found in the *Toldoth Yeshua,* see Krauss, p. 307, s. v. *Luft-Kampf.* It can hardly have been known to Christians, nor would they, even if they had been familiar with it, have thought of turning it into a term of abuse. Another version of the *Toldoth* in alluding to this incident says: " Wegen dieses Ereignisses weinen sie [die Christen] in ihrer Nacht [a pun on Weihnachten] und wegen der That, die Juda an ihm verübte."—Krauss, p. 55. From this it is clear that the author conceives the story as an insult to the followers of Christ. Only Hebrews could have employed the incident in a curse.

the gospel of the day and while the tapers were being extinguished to emphasize the solemnity of the scene, the officiating priest read from the pulpit these words:

> May they who refuse to obey be accursed, and have their portion with Cain the first murderer, with Judas the archtraitor, and with Dathan and Abiram, who went down alive into the pit. May they be accursed in the life that now is; and may their hope of salvation be put out, as the light of these candles is extinguished from their sight.[5]

An unusual form of the curse occurs in a Greek imprecation against the avaricious, which alludes to the fall of Judas from his lofty position:

> Εἴ τις οὖν θελήσει διὰ φιλοχρηματίαν ἢ δι' ἑτέραν αἰτίαν τινὰ καταφρονῆσαι τῶν ἐν τῷ παρόντι χρυσοβούλλῳ λόγῳ τῆς βασιλείας μου διωρισμένων, πρῶτα μὲν τὸ τῆς ἁγίας τριάδος φέγγος, ὅτε παριστάμεθα τῷ φοβερῷ βήματι, μὴ θεάσαιτο· ἐκπέσοι δὲ καὶ τῆς τῶν χριστιανῶν μερίδος, ὡς ὁ Ἰούδας τῆς δωδεκάδος.[6]

In an incident recounted by Gregory of Tours (c. 540-594) there appears something which resembles the Judas Iscariot curse and which perhaps belongs here. Bishop Praetextatus was being tried under the statute "Episcopus in homicidio, adulterio et periurio depraehensus, a sacerdotio divillatur," and failed to obtain the favor of King Chilpericus in his defense: "petiit rex, ut aut tonicam [sic] eius scinderetur, aut centesimus octavus psalmus, qui maledictionibus [sic] Scarioticas continet, super caput eius recitaretur"—or that it should be decreed against him that he could never receive communion.[7]

---

[5] E. C. Brewer, *The Historical Note-Book*, s. v. "Peace of God."

[6] This passage occurs in the "Aurea Bulla De Instrumentis Ecclesiarum" (1148 A. D.) of the emperor Manuel Comnenus; see *Jus graecoromanum, Pars III, Novellae constitutiones*, ed. Zachariae a Lingenthal, Lipsiae, 1857, Nov. LVI, pp. 443 ff. It is quoted with minor inaccuracies by Solovev, *K legendam ob Iudye predatelye*, Kharkov, 1898, p. 104, n. 1.

[7] *Historia Francorum*, lib. V (*Monumenta Germaniae Historica, Scriptores Rerum Merovingiarum*, I, i, p. 214). The 108th Psalm here alluded to is now the 109th; the early Fathers thought it referred prophetically to Judas, see, e. g., Origen, *Contra Celsum*, II, 20 (M. S. G., 11, 836-837); Wier (cols. 526 ff.) mentions the psalm particularly in connection with the curse as used against thieves, and Verdam in an excellent essay on charms in general cites a long formula "Ad

2. *Ecclesiastical Uses.* Martin remarks that the church rarely employs the Judas curse in the vernacular; and this might be expected, for the formal documents of the church are written almost without exception in Latin. His earliest Latin example dates from 908 A. D., and it is not until the thirteenth century that the curse is written in Spanish. To the eleventh century belongs a long and detailed Greek curse preserved in a set of regulations for a monastery. Since it refers to the hanging of Judas rather than to his lot in Hell, it belongs to a divergent form. In rhetorical effectiveness it does not suffer by comparison with the more familiar type:

Εἰ δέ τις παρὰ τὰ διατεταγμένα παρ' ἐμοῦ ἐπιχειρήσει τι διαπράξασθαι ἢ βασιλεὺς ἢ ἄρχων, εἴτε ἀρχόμενος, εἴτε ἀρχιερεὺς ἢ ἱερεὺς ἢ τι τῶν παρὰ τῆς ἐμῆς ἀρεσκείας ἐντεταλμένων παραβῆναι ἢ ἐφορείαν ὅλως ἐν αὐτοῖς ἐνθυμηθῆναι ἢ χαριστικάριον ἄλλον ἐπιστῆσαι ἢ προνοητὴν ἐκτὸς ὧν ἐγὼ μνημονεύσω, ἢ ἀναφορὰν ἢ προχείρισιν προστασίας τινός, (πάσης γὰρ ἐπισκοπῆς ὀρθοδόξων ὀφείλει μνημονεύειν ὁ τοῦ πτωχοτροφείου τοῦ Πανοικτίρμονος ναός), καταραθείη ὁ τοιοῦτος ἀπὸ θεοῦ παντοκράτορος καὶ ἐκριζωθείη ἐξ ἀνθρώπων ἡ μνήμη αὐτοῦ καὶ καταλάβοι αὐτὸν πένθος καὶ οὐαὶ καὶ προπορεύσοιτο αὐτοῦ θλῖψις, καὶ δοίη αὐτῷ κύριος ὁ θεὸς τὸν τρόμον τοῦ Κάϊν, τὴν λέπραν τοῦ Γιεζῆ, τὴν ἀγχόνην τοῦ Ἰούδα καὶ λογισθείη ἡ μερὶς αὐτοῦ μετ' ἐκείνων τῶν εἰπόντων· ἆρον ἆρον, σταύρωσον τὸν τοῦ θεοῦ υἱόν· καὶ μὴ ἴδοι ἐπ' αὐτὸν ἐν ἐλέει ὁ παντέφορος ὀφθαλμός, ἀλλ' ἐξαλειφθείη ἐκ γῆς τὸ μνημόσυνον αὐτοῦ καὶ κυριευθείη ὑπὸ πάντων τῶν ἐχθρῶν αὐτοῦ καὶ ἀπαντήσοι αὐτῷ αἰώνιος τιμωρία.[3]

cognoscendum furem" in which the psalm (but not Judas) is mentioned; see "Over Bezweringsformulieren," *Mededeelingen van de Maatschappij der nederlandsche Letterkunde te Leiden over het jaar 1900-1901*, Leiden, 1901, pp. 43-46. The history of the exegesis of this psalm and of its interpretation as prefiguring the death of Judas is of considerable interest.

[3] Michael Attaliates, Διάταξις, in Miklosich and Müller, *Acta et Diplomata Graeca Medii Aevi*, V (Vienna, 1887), pp. 300-301. It is also printed in Constantinus Sathas, Μεσαιωνικὴ βιβλιοθήκη, I (Venice, 1872), 12-13. See further W. Nissen, *Die Διάταξις des Michael Attaliates von 1077*, Jena Diss., 1894; he cites (p. 37) a list of parallels to this curse under the heading: "Schwere Fluchformeln gegen die Uebertreter seiner Vorschriften"; but it does not appear that any of these mention Judas. At the same place he gives also a number of parallels to the freedom of the monastery from secular or ecclesiastical superiors. The

Much later than these is a curious passage in a vernacular decree of the council at Moscow in 1667 which excommunicates schismatics in the following terms:

> And may he [who does not believe and who does not truly repent] be excommunicated and unforgiven until death, and may his lot and soul be with Judas Iscariot, the traitor, and with the Jews who mocked Christ, and with Arius, and with other accursed heretics.[9]

Notwithstanding the gap in space and time this clearly belongs to the same tradition as the usual Western curse: "habeat partem cum Iuda." The Russian oath seems also to follow the model of Michael Attaliates in referring to the Jews who cursed Christ; at any rate I do not find them mentioned in any Western curse.

In the upper Albanian diocese of Achrida (or Ochrida), which claimed and struggled to maintain *autocephalia* or ecclesiastical independence for more than a thousand years and which was alternately dominated by Latin and by Greek missionaries until the final abolition of its freedom by the orthodox patriarch in 1767, the Judas curse was officially employed on at least two occasions. It was appended to a pastoral letter written by the patriarch Joasaph and the synod in 1708. This example is interesting for its mention of the 318 Nicene fathers, who are found with some frequency in the near Eastern formulæ. It is directed against any one who may be led to speak scandal against the monastery and the priest's rulings:

"Ὅς δ' ἂν ἀνευλαβείᾳ καὶ αὐθαδείᾳ οἰστρηλατούμενος κινήσῃ τι σκάνδαλον κατὰ τοῦ ψυχωφελοῦς καὶ θεαρέστου τούτου ἔργου τοῦ φροντιστηρίου καὶ ποιήσῃ τι παρὰ τὰ διορισθέντα καὶ διαταχθέντα παρὰ τῆς αὐτοῦ ἐνδοξότητος καὶ κοινῇ ψήφῳ ἡμῶν καὶ συνοδικῇ ἀποφάσει ἐπικυρωθέντα, ὁποῖός ἐστιν ὁ τοιοῦτος, ἱερωμένος ἢ λαϊκός, συγγενὴς τῆς αὐτοῦ ἐνδοξότητος ἢ ξένος, ἐγχώριος ἢ ἐξ ἀλλοδαπῆς, ἀφωρισμένος ἄῃ ἀπὸ θεοῦ κυρίου παντοκράτορος καὶ κατηραμένος καὶ ἀσυγχώρητος καὶ ἄλυτος μετὰ θάνατον. αἱ πέτραι καὶ ὁ σίδηρος λυθήσονται, αὐτὸς δὲ οὐδαμῶς· καὶ ἄῃ στένων καὶ τρέμων ἐπὶ γῆς ὡς ὁ Κάϊν· κληρονομήσοι τὴν λέπραν τοῦ Γιεζῆ καὶ τὴν ἀγχόνην τοῦ Ἰούδα.

Διάταξις seems to be a very interesting document for the student of folk-lore and mediæval custom; cf. Krumbacher, *Byz. Litt²*., pp. 269-271, 315, 317 or the *Catholic Encyclopedia*, II, 60.

[9] Quoted by Solovev (p. 104) from *Materialy dlya raskola za pervoe vremya ego suščestvovaniya*, Moscow, 1876, II, 219-220.

THE JUDAS CURSE.

τὰ πράγματα καὶ οἱ κόποι αὐτοῦ ἄησαν εἰς ἐξολόθρευσιν καὶ ἀφανισμόν· καὶ προκοπὴν οὐ μὴ ἴδοι, ἔχων καὶ τὰς ἀρὰς τῶν ἁγίων τριακοσιων δέκα καὶ ὀκτὼ θεοφόρων πατέρων τῶν ἐν Νικαίᾳ καὶ τῶν λοιπῶν ἁγίων συνόδων.[10]

It seems pretty clear that the curse—at least as it was used in this diocese—was a rather formal thing which did not permit of much variation from the accepted norm. Thus a decade later a very similar oath forms the conclusion of a pastoral letter of the patriarch Kyr Zosimas in which he acknowledges a gift to a school in Kastoria and promises the donor the protection of the patriarch and of the synod. The letter is dated 1719. The curse is as follows:

Ἐπὶ τέλους δέ, εἰ μὲν ἱερώμενος τύχῃ ὤν, ἐν ἁγίῳ πνεύματι ἀποφαινόμεθα μετὰ πάσης τῆς ἱερᾶς συνόδου, ἵνα γυμνοῦται τῆς ἱερατικῆς αὐτοῦ τάξεως καὶ ἱεροπραξίας, καὶ παντελῶς νὰ καθαίρηται (sic) καὶ νὰ ἀναθεματίζεται καὶ νὰ ἀποστρέφεται ὑπὸ πάντων τῶν εὐσεβῶν καὶ ὀρθοδόξων χριστιανῶν, ὡς ὁ προδότης Ἰούδας, καὶ νὰ καταδιώκεται ὡς λυμεὼν τῆς πατρίδος καὶ κοινότητος· εἰ δὲ λαϊκός, ἐστὶ ἀφωρισμένος παρὰ κυρίου παντοκράτορος, κατηραμένος καὶ ἀσυγχώρητος καὶ ἄλυτος μετὰ θάνατον· αἱ πέτραι καὶ ὁ σίδηρος λυθήσονται, αὐτὸς δὲ οὐδαμῶς· κληρονομήσῃ τὴν λέπραν τοῦ Γιεζῆ καὶ τὴν ἀγχόνην τοῦ Ἰούδα, ὡς ἄλλος $\bar{β}$ Ἰούδας· νὰ σχισθῇ ἡ γῆ καὶ νὰ τὸν καταπίῃ, ὡς τὸν Δαθὰν καὶ Ἀβηρών· νὰ τρέμῃ καὶ ἀναστενάξῃ, ὡς ὁ Κάϊν, καὶ αὐτὸς καὶ τὰ παιδία του καὶ ἡ γυναῖκα του· τὸ μέρος του νὰ εἶνε μὲ τοὺς Ἰουδαίους, ὁποῦ ἐσταύρωσαν τὸν κύριον τῆς δόξης.[11]

3. *Legal Uses.* In documents recording gifts or sales of land, the Judas curse often appears; but the fact that the imprecation is usually in Latin, even when the deed is in the vernacular, shows that this clause had become a stereotyped formula. Martin has cited a considerable variety of forms, which bespeaks some freedom in its use. An early example which is mentioned in connection with a gift of Theodetrudes to the monastery of St. Denis in 627 is interesting because of the rhetorical skill in its management:

Propterea rogo et contestor coram Deo et Angelis eius et omni natione hominum tam propinquis quam extraneis, ut nullus contra

---

[10] H. Gelzer, "Der Patriarchat von Achrida," *Abhandlungen der königlichen sächsischen Gesellschaft der Wissenschaften*, XLVII (phil.-hist. Klasse, XX), Leipzig, 1902, Part 5, p. 73. He cites another example (which I have not seen) in Ἱεροσ. σταχ., II, p. 325.

[11] Gelzer, p. 93.

deliberationem meam impedimentum S. Dionysio de hac re facere praesumat; si fuerit, quia manus suas ad hoc apposuerit faciendo, aeternus rex peccata mea absolvat et ille maledictus in inferno inferiori et anathema et Maranatha percussus cum Juda cruciandis descendat, et peccatum quem amittit in filios et in domo sua crudelissime plaga ut leprose pro huius culpa a Deo percussus, ut non sit qui inhabitet in Domo eius, ut eorum plaga in multis timorem concutiat, et quantum res ipsa meliorata valuerit, duplex satisfactione fisco egenti exsolvat."

King Eadgar's charter of liberties to Taunton (968 A. D.), which is mentioned but not quoted by Martin, is particularly interesting because the Latin text is accompanied with a briefer, free Anglo-Saxon translation:

Si quis autem praesumptuosus, diabolo instigante, hanc libertatem infringere, minuereve, vel in aliud quam constituimus transferre voluerit, anathema sit, et in Christi maledictione permanens aeterno barathri incendio, cum Iuda Christi proditore ejusque complicibus miserrimus puniatur.

Sy he mid awurgednesse ascyred fram ures Drihtnes gemanan and ealra his halgena, and on helle susle ecelice getintragod mid Iudan þe Christes lewa wes."

A score of instances, exemplifying the uses of the Judas curse in the province—then the kingdom—of León, can be picked out from a single collection of charters of gift and similar documents.[14] All of them fall between the years 918 and 1034, the limits of the collection. The earliest of these curses (in a deed of Ordoño II to the monastery of Eslonza in 918) is as follows:

Si quis sane temerarius et audax ad inrumpendum conaverit venire, presenti seculo non careat humana vel divina ultionem, et in futuro piceam cum transgressoribus possideat penam et cum Iuda proditore finitis temporibus sit [so]ciaturus.

---

[12] Félibien, *Histoire de St. Denys*, Pièces justificatives, No. 2, as cited by Crttwell, " Die Verfluchung der Bücherdiebe," *Archiv für Kulturgeschichte*, IV (1906), 207-208.

[13] Benjamin Thorpe, *Diplomatarium Anglicum Aevi Saxonici*, London, 1865, pp. 234-235. By a slip of the pen Martin ascribes another Anglo-Saxon example of the curse to Queen Æthelred. Her name should be Queen Æthelflæd (the first wife of Æthelred II [the Unready], 978-1016).

[14] Barrau-Dihigo, " Chartes royales léonaises," *Revue hispanique*, X (1903), 356 ff. It will not be necessary to give a page reference for each example, since the year will afford a sufficient identification.

THE JUDAS CURSE.

Three years later the clause which becomes a standard form —if any form may be so termed—makes its appearance:

> Quod si quisquam ex aliqua generis homo voluerit hanc nostram violare firmitatem, anathematicetur per secula cuncta, et luat penas cum Iuda Domini traditore eterna dampnacione, et ne immunis a dampna secularia videatur, exsolvet quod inquietaverit in duplo et insuper decem libras auri vobis perpetim profuturas.

Characteristic of this are the words "luat penas cum Iuda" which reappear again and again throughout these curses and show a supremacy which is only feebly contested from 960 by a new and more verbose formula. A long curse of 941 is curious for its unusual phrases and still more so for the fact that after more than a generation it is copied verbatim in a similar document of the same monastery. This queer wordy affair must have caught some monk's fancy and when it was his turn to draft a deed he copied the old formula:

> Si quis sane ex successoribus nostris vel cuiuslibet alicuius persona, potentior aut inferior, hoc factum nostrum infringere quiverit, quicumque ille fuerit, sit excommunicatus et perpetua confusione multatus in conspectu Dei patris omnipotentis et sanctorum angelorum, apostolorum et martyrum eius, et insuper cum Iuda Domini proditore uno contubernetur in loco in tenebris exterioribus et caligosis, atque pariet tantum et aliut tantum quantum infringere quiverit, et hec scriptura plenam abeat firmitatem.[18]

The imprecation which embellishes the gift of Sancho I to the monastery of Sahagun in 960 is the first to mention the patron saints of the foundation—they occur with considerable regularity in the later curses written at this place—and is couched in an unusually rhetorical style:

> Quod si aliquis huius nostre hoblationis temerare presumpserit et huius serie testamenti nostre infringere maluerit, obto, obto per intercessionem patronum meorum Sanctorum Facundi et Primitivi, ille temerator a sinu matris ecclesie seclusum existere, et eternis incendiis cum proditore Christi faciant illum cremare, ultimi examinationis diem non cum celestis paratum possideat gaudium, sed cum reprobis eat in ignem eternum qui diabolo et angelis eius est preparatum, et in corpore vivens propriis careat lucernis a fronte, aures denegent auditum et lingua loquendi careat usum.

---

[18] This is in a deed of Ramiro II to the monastery of Celanova (*Revue hispanique*, X, 377); compare with it a deed to the same monastery of 985, *ibid.*, p. 425.

Here first appears the phrase "careat lucernis a fronte" which becomes very frequent in the later curses. It recurs, for example, in a document of 968:

> Si quis autem ex prosapia nostra genusque regale, tam religiosus quam laicus, seu quislibet humani generis homo, hunc votum litationis nostre infringere vel minuere seu inmutare temptaverit, atque post discessum nostrum hanc regiam tenuerit sedem, quicquid talia egerit, inprimis a fronte careat lucernis corpusque eius vermibus scaturiat, et cum sceleratis penas luat tartareas numquam finiendas, et cum Iuda crudelis et Domini proditore sors existat in eternam damnationem, et hanc seriem testamenti quam pro remedio animarum nostrarum fieri elegimus, in cunctis obtineat firmitatis rovorem evo perhenni et usque in finem venturam.

Observe in this the reminiscence of the "luat penas." In 971 the phrase reads: "et cum Iuda proditore multetur penas in eterna dampnacione," and it is very freely handled in a clause of 975:

> Si quis igitur deinc et in subsequentibus temporibus, tan ex clericis quan ex laycis vel cuiuspia omo asertionis, contra unc factum meum inrumpere vel inmutare temtaberit, inprimis sit excomunicatus et a sacro corpus Domini sit extraneo, ac post mortem cum Iuda qui Dominum tradidit in infernum perpetim lugeat, insuper eveniat super eum omnes maledictiones que scriptas sunt in libro Moysi, et pro temporali pena pariet duo auri talenta, et anc scriptura plenan abeat firmitate.

In imprecations of 977 and 980 the clause appears with comparatively slight changes. In 986 it is used in conjunction with the "a fronte careat lucernis":

> Si quis tamen . . . infringere, disrumpere aut disturbare vel extraneare voluerit, inprimis communione corporis et sanguinis Christi, qui est redemptio nostra, extraneus maneat, propriis a fronte careat lucernis, atque cum Iuda Domini proditore anathematus et picea tunica indutus in inferni baratro penas lugeat eternas, et a regia hordinatione vel iussione quoartatus, pariare quogatur iuxta gotdigam legem auri talenta quinque, et quod desuper scriptum resonat duplare non tardet.

The half-dozen curses which occur in the last fifty years of the period 918-1034 show that systematization had taken place, and as a result all but one contain the clause " et cum Iuda Domini proditore penas semper lugeat infinitas " (988), or, as the last instance (1034) reads, " et cum Iuda Domini proditore luat penas in eterna dampnacione." By this time—the first quarter of the eleventh century—the Judas curse had become, so far as the Leonese charters are concerned, an empty, meaningless formula, crystallized in a set phrase. The one imprecation (of 994) which varies from the norm lacks the spirit and zest of the oaths of the earlier generation and only emphasizes the seeming loss of interest in the Judas curse:

> Si quis vero quippiam homo . . . exurgere voluerit, ut hanc testationem convellere atque confringere presumat, inprimis sit excomunicatus et perpetua maledictione constrictus, in conspectu Dei Patris omnipotentis et sanctorum omnium angelorum eius sit coram Filio eius Sanctoque Spiritu obnoxius et reus et a cunctorum sanctorum cetu extraneus, atque cum reprobis et condemnatis eternos ignes suscipiatur de stabili in iatu, sive sit vir, sive mulier, multiplicentur tenebras tenebre illius et mors morti eius atque Domini proditoris damna sortitus una mancipentur in pena, et insuper damna temporalia afflictus duplet tantum quantum de hoc testamento aufferre voluerit, et vobis perpetim abitura.

An imprecation used to protect a gift from a French monastery in 1053 is remarkable for its mention of Nero, who does not figure so frequently in this collection of villains:

> Si quis autem huic largitioni meae contraire aut minuere ex hac re quippiam temptaverit, maledictione Cham, qui patris pudenda deridenda fratribus ostendit, feriatur, et cum Dathan et Abiron, quos terra vivos absorbuit, et cum Juda traditore, qui se suspendit laqueo, et cum Nerone, qui Petrum in cruce suspendit et Paullum decollavit, nisi resipuerit et ad satisfactionibus remedium confugerit, cum diabolo in inferno poenas luat, donec abiturus veniam eum diabolus est accepturus. Amen.[16]

In some Slavic deeds to monasteries the Judas curse is found in the vernacular. Thus in a document recording a gift of Stefan Detchanskij in 1327: "And may he be counted with Judas and with those who said, 'His blood on us and on our children.'" [17] And similarly in a deed of Stefan Dushan: "And

---

[16] Guerard, *Cartulaire de S. Père*, I, 222, as cited by Crüwell, *Archiv für Kulturgeschichte*, IV (1906), 208 from Montalembert, *Die Mönche des Abendlandes* (tr. Müller), VI, 42.

[17] Šafarik, *Památky drevniho pisemnistni jiho slovanův, vydáni druhe*, 1873, p. 99 (quoted by Solovev, p. 192). The original is: i da iest pričten' s' iyudoyu i rekšikh: kr'v' iego na nas' i na čedekh našikh. [This and other examples credited to Šafarik are taken from Solovev, since Šafarik's book is inaccessible to me.]

may he be counted with Judas the betrayer of Christ and with those who said: 'His blood on us and our children.'"[18] Arius is mentioned in a deed of St. Lazar: "And may he be counted with Judas and Arius and those, who said: 'His blood on us and on our children.'"[19] Similar imprecations are noted twice by Solovev in the documents of the Bulgarian emperor, Jan Šišman: "And may he share the lot of Judas the betrayer of the Lord, and inherit the leprosy of Gehazi" or "May he have the lot of Judas and Arius."[20] Solovev comments: "It is curious that Judas is mentioned alone in the earlier deeds and in the later [we find] Judas and Arius. How is this to be explained? Is it impossible to find an explanation in the history of the South Slavic church? I have not enough material to decide this question." It is hardly necessary to look for a reason in the church history of a particular nation; as time passed the heresy of Arius was more and more generally and severely denounced by Athanasians. The same curse is found in France, e. g., "cum Iuda Scarioth Caifanque, Arrio atque Sabellio in inferno penas sustineat" or "cum Iuda proditore et Simone Mago et Arrio et Sabellio et Aman et Oloferno demergatur in inferno" (Martin, p. 436, n. 1).

4. *Special Uses against Thieves.* John Wier, who wrote a long treatise on witches at the end of the sixteenth century, terms the Judas curse "anathema sancti Adalberti"[21] and de-

---

[18] Šafarik, p. 103: i da ie pričten' iyude predatelyu Khristovu i tem rekšiim': kr'v' ego na nas' i na čedekh' našikh'.

[19] Šafarik, p. 108: i da ie pričten' iyude i arii i tem, iže rekoša: krov' ego na nas i na čedekh našikh.

[20] Šafarik, p. 109: i pričestīe da imat' s iyudoą predatelem gospodinem, i prokazą glezīvą do nasleduet'; and: i s' iyudę i arię česti da zimat.

[21] To Professor Hepding of Giessen I am indebted for the suggestion that the "anathema S. Adalberti" may not refer to the famous saint but to Bishop Adalbert or Aldebert who was condemned as a heretic in 745 at the instance of Boniface. (See Herzog-Hauck, *Realencyklopädie d. Theologie;* the documentary account may be found in Schannat and Hartzheim, *Concilia Germaniae,* I, 60 ff.) This Adelbert or Aldebert was honored by the folk as a saint. He circulated a "Himmelsbrief" and a prayer in which the names of angels occurred and which the Pope termed devilish. The recollection of his magical powers persisted among the folk and his name may very easily have become attached to such a formula as the Judas curse. Professor Hepding remarks that he

clares that its use to regain stolen property is open to condemnation as impiety. He then gives with some comment a very elaborate curse (and charm) of 112 short lines, which is briefly as follows:

> Ex authoritate Dei omnipotentis ... sancti Adalberti & omnium Confessorum ... excommunicamus, damnamus, maledicimus uinculo anathematis, & à liminibus sanctæ matris Ecclesiæ segregamus illos fures, sacrilegos ... sit pars eorum cum Dathan & Abiron, quos terra propter eorum peccata & superbiam deglutiuit: sit etiam pars illorum cum Iuda traditore, qui Dominum precio uendidit, Amen: & cum Pontio Pilato, & cum eis qui dixerunt Domino Deo, Recede à nobis, uiarum tuarum scientiam nolumus: fiant filij eorum orphani: sint maledicti in ciuitate ... maledictum caput eorum, ora, nares ... uiscera omnia. ... Adiuro te Lucifer cum omnibus satellitibus tuis, cum Patre & Filio & Spiritu sancto, & cum humanitate & natiuitate Christi, & cum uirtute omnium sanctorum, ut nullam habeas requiem diebus neque noctibus, donec perducas eos ad interitum ... & sicut Dominus beato Petro apostolo & eius successoribus, quorum uices tenemus, & nobis quamuis indignis potestatem contulit ... & sicut candela de manib. meis eiecta extinguitur, sic opera eorum & animæ eorum in foetore barathri extinguentur, nisi reddant quod furati sunt, infra certum terminum.[*]

The omitted passages are simply expansions or variations of the preceding ideas. Wier found particularly offensive the fact that Lucifer and his satellites are called upon along with the powers of light: "Quae communio Christo cum Belial?" (2 Cor. 6) he observes. Furthermore, Christ gave Peter the keys of Heaven (Matth. 16), but not the right to blaspheme: "Non blasphemorum eiusmodi anathematum fulmina concessit, multo minus mandauit." These opinions concerning the Judas curse (as employed against thieves) seem to have been held with some tenacity, for Frommann in his curious volume *De Fascinatione Magica* of about a century later digests the objections as follows:

> De hoc anathemate quid sit judicandum Freudius *Quaest.* 221 ex Brochmanno & aliis Theologis proponit ita: In hoc anathemate (1) fur

---

later found that this suggestion of his had been anticipated. M. Delrio in the *Disquisitionum magicarum libri VI* comments as follows: Alii utuntur exorcismo seu anathemate, quod blaspheme vocant S. Adalberti. ... Quam prorsus suspicor esse illius Adelberti haeretici, qui se sanctum vocabat et damnatus fuit à Papa Zacharia. (Mains edition, 1624, p. 469.)

[*] J. Wierus, *De praestigiis daemonum*, Basel, 1583, cols. 522-524, lib. V, cap. vi, "Ut Res furto sublata restituatur, anathema magicum."

æternæ morti, & damnationi adjudicatur, cum Christianus etiam inimicis bene precari debeat, Matth. 5. 44. quod contra naturam anathematis est, cujus finis est, ut homo carne afflictus salvetur in die adventus Jesu Christi 1. Cor. 5 (2) junctim invocatur S. Trinitas, Maria, Apostoli &c. quod Idololatria est (3) junctim quoque adjuratur Lucifer, & Deus & uterque in vindictam pari jure imploratur, quod est colere Diabolum, & Deum abnegare, Deo simul & Diabolo servire, communionem Christi & Belial introducere."

This employment of the Judas curse is particularly interesting because the curse was traditionally used as a protection against book-thieves. From the association of Judas with thievery, which was already present in every one's mind, and which was reinforced by this imprecation and the accepted exegesis of Psalm 109, there arose a curious charm which compares the sufferings of Judas at the betrayal to the sufferings invoked upon the thief's head and by means of these pains it is hoped that he will be forced to return the stolen goods.[24] An anathema of the bishop of Czernowitz in 1786 makes the development of the Judas charm against thieves clearer. Dosothei, by the grace of God Bishop of the imperial Bukovina, learned that one Theodor Halip, priest in the village of Oprischeni, had lost by theft four oxen, one mare, and one heifer, and that further the villager Basil Stratulat had complained of the disappearance of eleven horses and six oxen. Since his soul " could not endure these injuries and the despicable sins of these thefts, which had been committed by wretched people without fear of God," he cursed the guilty ones and their accomplices by virtue of the power entrusted to him by God and our Savior (this is the clause at which Wier and Frommann balked) in the following fashion:

That all of them—thieves and accomplices—should be cursed by God the Lord, the just Judge and Savior, Jesus Christ, by His most pure mother, by the twelve apostles, by the 318 fathers of the council at Nicaea, and all saints. Iron, ore, and stone and all hard substances should decay, but their bodies should persist uninjured and undissolved after death! In eternity their souls should partake with Judas of eternal torments, but in this world the wrath of God should rest upon them and be poured over them and their children! They should have

---

[23] J. C. Frommann, *Tractatus de fascinatione Novus et Singularis*, Norimbergae, 1675, pp. 708-709.

[24] See my paper, "Judas Iscariot in Charms and Incantations," *Washington University Studies*, VIII (1920), Humanistic Series, 1, 3-17.

no success in life, their labors and efforts should accomplish their destruction. . . . The tremor of Cain and the sores of Gehazi should cling to their bodies. . . . Those who know and disclose the evildoers shall be pardoned, and they shall be blessed by God, the Lord. So may it be."

A queer formula employed against thieves which was written down in a German recipe-book in Baden in 1727 is half anathema and half spell. Beginning with an allusion of magical flavor, it continues with a phrase intentionally reminiscent of the powers conferred on St. Peter (Matth. 16: 19) and its conclusion is likewise half incantation and half curse. Noteworthy is the comparison of successive states of the thief's mind to successive states of Judas' mind at the betrayal. This apparently unusual formula is as follows:

Ich beschwöre dich bey Maister Arbegast, der allen dieben ein Maister was, der sei bundten und knipft und nimmermer auffgelöst biss ahn jüngsten tag. da soll dir so bandt sein als dem Judas wahr, da er unser lieber herr Jesus Christus verkaufft hat, so bandt sol dir sein dieb und diebin; wan du wüllt stehlen das mein, so solst du gefangen und gebunden sein; da solt so wenig ruoh haben als Judas hat, da er unserm lieben herrn Jesum Christum einen falschen kuss gab, so bang sol dir sein dieb. . . . Du dieb oder diebin solt wenig weichen von meinem guot, biss dass du mir kannst zehlen die staudten, die über die erden ausluogen, du muost mir bei meinem guoth still stahn, biss unser liebe frau ein andren Sohn gebehrt und ich dich in des Teuffels namen urlaub geb im nahmen Gottes vatters und des Sohnes und des hl. Gaists. amen."

5. *Special Uses against Book Thieves.* Ecclesiastics in the Levant and in Europe used various imprecations, some of them containing the name of Judas, to protect the books of their libraries from theft. Crüwell, who has collected the continental examples,[27] believes that they were suggested originally by the

---

[25] Kaindl, "Beiträge zur Volkskunde Osteuropas," *Zeitschrift des Vereins für Volkskunde*, XXVII (1917), 240-241, No. 20, "Fluchbrief gegen Diebe" (quoted from F. A. Wickenhauser, *Geschichte des Bistums Radautz*, I, 191 ff.).

[26] Birlinger, "Volkstümliches aus der Baar [Baden]," *Alemannia*, II (1875), 128, No. 4.

[27] "Die Verfluchung der Bücherdiebe," *Archiv für Kulturgeschichte*, IV (1906), 197-223. That the book-curse has not yet outlived its former usefulness is apparent from the experience of Gelzer, who had difficulty in obtaining a manuscript that had been stolen from the

author's curse against the falsifiers of his text. The damnation threatened against the stealer of a book is a corollary to the notion that the copier of a manuscript had earned a claim on eternal happiness; and in their beginnings, says Crüwell, the expression of the one idea is roughly contemporary with that of the other. The Church took no decided position in the matter, in particular it did not definitely favor the use of curses to prevent the theft of books, and consequently some monasteries never made use of them. Others seem to have a tradition of some antiquity favoring the curse. The fashion of the Judas curse in this use seems to have originated, so far as the Occident is concerned, at Monte Cassino, the oldest of the Benedictine monasteries, and to have spread from there into the Benedictine monasteries of France. On the first page of a ninth-century manuscript of the *Historia tripartita* of Cassiodorus belonging to Monte Cassino the thief is cursed in this way:

Si quis nobis hunc librum quolibet modo malo ingenio tollere temptauerit aut uoluerit, sit anathema maranatha, et cum Juda traditore domini triginta maledictiones iuxta numerum triginta argenteorum quibus dominum uendidit quae in centesimo octauo psalmo scriptae reperiuntur. Has omnes maledictiones et hic et in aeternum possideat, qui hunc ut dictum est nobis tollere maluerit.[28]

The standard Benedictine curse is, however, shorter and makes no mention of the 109th (formerly 108th) Psalm, which was thought to prefigure the fate of Judas. In the Benedictine monasteries of eastern France (Tours, St. Mesmin de Micy, St. Fleury) the formula seems to have run much as follows:

Hic est liber Sancti Benedicti abbatis Floriacensis coenobii; si quis eum aliquo ingenio non redditurus abstraxerit, cum Juda proditore, Anna et Caipha atque Pilato damnationem accipiat! Amen.[29]

---

monastery. See his account in "Der wiederaufgefundene Kodex des hl. Klemens," *Berichte über die Verhandlungen d. k. sächs. Gesell. d. Wiss. zu Leipzig*, Phil.-hist. Klasse, LV (1903) p. 61.

[28] A. Reifferscheid, "Bibliotheca Patrum Latinorum Italica, V-IX," *Sitzungsberichte der Wiener Akademie, phil.-hist. Klasse*, LXXI (1872), 88.

[29] Cf. Crüwell, p. 214; L. Delisle, *Catalogue des manuscrits des fonds Libri et Barrois*, p. 30. The example above is taken from MS. Fonds Libri 92 (now Bibliothèque Nationale, Nouv. acq. lat. 1597), a collection of extracts from St. Gregory in an eighth-century hand. A slightly

Ludwig Traube has collated 28 manuscripts which once belonged to the monastery of St. Mesmin de Micy in order to arrive at a "critical" text of the curse, which does not vary essentially from that above (19 of his examples contain the "cum Juda").[30] The manuscripts of the Benedictine monastery of St. Victor in Paris contained, says Crüwell, the Judas curse. It is also to be found, according to Traube, in a manuscript of St. Martin of Tours which is now in England (MS Egerton 2831). The combination of Ananias, Caiaphas, and Judas occurs also in the Brendan legend, where it may have been suggested by the oath.[30a]

Brief and to the point is a rhyming curse in an old German manuscript: "Qui te furetur, cum Juda dampnificetur." [31]

I have noted two examples of the Judas curse against book thieves in Greek,—enough to show that others undoubtedly exist. These are particularly important since they are separated by several centuries, one being of the early eleventh century, the other of the fourteenth. In form they, like the other Greek and Levantine examples, differ sufficiently from the Latin type to prove that they represent a parallel tradition rather than a translation from a Western formula. The continued existence of this parallel tradition may be demonstrated by a comparison between the anathema of Bishop Dosothei cited above and the second of these Greek book-curses; observe in both the mention of the three hundred eighteen Nicene Fathers, who are not found in the Western formulæ. The earlier of the two curses occurs in a manuscript of Symeon Metaphrastes, dated in the colophon A. D. 1105:

Ὅστις οὖν βουληθῇ ἆραι τήνδε τὴν βίβλον ἀπὸ ταύτης τῆς μονῆς, ἢ εὐλόγως ἢ ἀνευλόγως . . . . . πρῶτον μὲν κληρονομείτω ἀνάθεμα, τὴν ἀρὰν τῶν ἁγίων θεοφόρων πατέρων, καὶ ἡ μερὶς αὐτοῦ μετὰ Ἰούδα τοῦ καὶ προδότου καὶ τῶν λοιπῶν ἀποστατῶν.[32]

different curse in Martène, *Voyage littéraire de deux religieux Bénédictins de Ste. Maur*, Paris, 1717, p. 68 omits Pilate and reads "portionem aeternae damnationis." The writer says that it headed a ninth-century book of sacraments.

[30] *Hieronymi chronicorum cod. Flor.*, p. xvi.

[30a] On Judas in the Brendan story see Dr. Paull F. Baum's *Judas' Sunday Rest*, which is to appear in the Modern Language Review.

[31] Wattenbach, *Schriftwesen*, 3rd ed., p. 528 (Hoffmann von Fallersleben, *Altdeutsche Handschriften*, p. 232).

[32] B. de Montfaucon, *Palaeographia Graeca, sive de ortu et progressu literarum Graecarum*, Paris, 1708, pp. 57-58, Codex Colbertinus 25. The monastery was in Constantinople.

Codex Colbertinus 10, of the fourteenth century, containing an *Interpretatio in Psalmos,* ends with the following curse:

Εἴτις τοῦτο [the volume] ἐξαιρήσῃ ἄνευ τὴν γνώμην τοῦ Ἀρχιτάτα ἡμῶν, νὰ ἔχῃ τὴν θείαν καὶ ζωοποιὸν καὶ ἀσύγχυτον καὶ ἀδιαίρετον τριάδα, καὶ τὴν παναγίαν τοῦ αὐτοῦ μητέρα, τοῦ τιμίου ἐνδόξου προφήτου προδρόμου καὶ βαπτιστοῦ Ἰωάννου, τῶν τιη. θεοφόρων πατέρων, καὶ πάντων σου [?] τῶν ἀγίων ἀμοιβήν, καὶ νὰ τὸν καταξεὸ (sic) ἐν Σοδομογομόρρας ω ἀγχόνι Ἰούδα ἀνάθεμα.[23]

In a Syriac manuscript in the St. Petersburg Public Library there is a remarkable passage which indicates that the Judas curse was known in the Levant in a form practically identical with that current in the West. The following words are written in Arabic letters on the fly-leaf:

This blessed book belongs to the church of the monastery of Sinai, and whosoever takes it away or tears a leaf from it, may the Virgin be a foe to him and may his fate be one with the fate of Judas Iscariot.[24]

This example is not dated by Solovev, but the curse appears again in a very similar form in an Arabic manuscript which is ascribed for palæographic reasons to the fourteenth century. The manuscript in question, containing New Testament Apocrypha, belongs to the convent of Deyr-es-Suriani or St. Mary Deipara in the Wady Natrôn, Egypt. In it a colophon, which is inserted at the end of the "Martyrdom of St. Andrew," runs as follows:

And praise be to God ever and always. This blessed book is the enduring perpetual guarded inheritance of the Monastery of Our Lady, the Lady whose lord is Anba Bishai, and is known as the Syrian Fathers. And no man shall have power from the Lord—praise be to Him!—to take it out of the Monastery on any pretence or by way of

---

[23] Montfaucon, pp. 75-78. "Hæc Græco-barbara, imo penitus Barbara," says Montfaucon, "hunc sensum habent: *si quis eum sine Archipapæ nutu abstulerit, incurrat maledictionem sanctæ Trinitatis, sanctæ Deiparæ, S. Joan. Baptistæ, SS. 318. Patrum Nicænorum et omnium Sanctorum, sortem Sodomæ et Gomorrhæ, laqueum Judæ, anathema.*" Though the Greek is not the best Attic, one may suspect that some of the blame attaches to the editor; the "[sic]" is his, and apparently a few more are needed; the "[?]" is mine.

[24] Solovev, p. 104, n. 1 (quoted from *Otčet Imperat. Pub. Bibl.* 1883, p. 184).

loss. And after he shall have taken it out his lot shall be with Judas, the betrayer of his Lord. And it was written for God's sake by permission of our Father, the Metropolitan Abbot of the Monastery above mentioned. And praise be to God always and for ever."

6. *Literary Uses.* Examples of the literary employment of the Judas curse are extremely rare.[36] Martin notes but three, all from the Spanish chronicles and romances, "where heroic style prevailed and conventionality was in order." An instance earlier than any of these may perhaps be seen in an allusion by Gregory of Tours to the 108th Psalm (now the 109th) and its interpretation as forecasting the fate of Judas. He says in the *Vita S. Abbadi:* if any one doubts his testimony, "et hic et in aeternum per virtutes sancti et beati domini Martini sit excommunicatus et anathematizatus, et veniat illa maledictio, quam psalmus CVIII continet in Judam Scariotis."[37] The solemnity of the oath is much emphasized in the *Klage* of Hartmann von Aue, one of the first of the great mediaeval German poets (fl. 1190). Here it is accompanied with a formal gesture, and the context indicates that it was spoken. The passage is as follows:

> Ich hân die vinger ûf geleit
> unde swer dir's einen eit:
> ich bite mir got helfen sô,
> daz ich iemer werde vrô
> oder iemer gewinne
> deheine werltminne
> oder dehein êre,
> niwan daz ich mit sêre
> müeze leiten mîn leben
> und dem ein unreht ende geben
> und daz diu arme sêle mîn
> êweclîchen müeze sîn
> in der tiefen helle
> Jûdases geselle,

---

[35] Agnes S. Lewis, *Horae Semiticae*, IV, "The Mythological Acts of the Apostles," London, 1904, p. 29.

[36] Polixenes' oath in the *Winter's Tale* may possibly be descended from the traditional form. He swears that Hermione is virtuous; calling down on his head these consequences if he speaks falsely:

> O, then my best blood turn
> To an infected jelly, and my name
> Be yoked with his that did betray the Best!
> —Act I, sc. ii, 417.

[37] M. S. L. 71, 1149.

> dâ nieman fröude haben mac,
> unz an den jungesten tac,
> und daz sî dannoch niht ensî
> vor des tiuvels banden frî.[38]

There is at least one instance of literary employment of the Judas curse in the Near East. In an Armenian version of the Debate of the Body and Soul the body counsels the soul to seek worldly pleasures. The soul recommends a very different course of life and "curses the body with the imprecation of Cain and Judas," but the body is unheeding.[39]

Into such various languages as Old Church Slavic, Russian, Arabic, and Armenian the Judas curse has made its way—a distribution which accords well with the fact that its first reported use was Justinian's exaction of it from his officials. Although it was widely used—and its employment in the vernacular seems to have been rather more frequent in the Eastern Empire than in the Western—it is nonetheless a bookish imprecation, transmitted by the Church and most often found in connection with the Church, its affairs and its belongings. In the West it seems later not to be highly regarded—compare the German chronicler Menckenius with the Middle High German poet,—but in the East I have observed no evidence of its comparative importance. There it was doubtless used for what it may have been worth.

ARCHER TAYLOR.

THE GALLOWS OF JUDAS ISCARIOT

ARCHER TAYLOR
Associate Professor of German

St. Matthew, with a reminiscence perhaps of Ahitophel's death, says that Judas committed suicide by hanging himself. But in failing to record what *sort* of tree the traitor chose he left a lacuna for later tradition to fill. This uncertainty might, indeed, be settled if there were any agreement among those travellers who have in later times been fortunate enough to see the tree itself. For as recently as the last century the guides have pointed it out; and its picture may be found in a popular magazine of the day.[1] But there is no unanimity here — even the testimony of Sir John Mandeville is not to be trusted — and it seems inevitable that this detail must remain in apocryphal doubt.[2] The Scotch, moreover, thinking of the scarcity of trees north of the Tweed, say that "Had Judas betrayed Christ in Scotland he might have repented before he could have found a tree to hang himself on."[3] And the Little Russians have the notion that the leaves of all trees

---

[1] *Popular Science Monthly*, XCIV (April, 1919), 33.

[2] The traditions have been collected by a number of scholars: Creizenach, *Beiträge zur Geschichte der deutschen Sprache*, II (1876), 183; de Gubernatis, *Mythologie des plantes*, II (Paris, 1882), 192-94 (his material is used with some modifications and enlargement by Folkard, *Plant Lore, Legends, and Lyrics*, London, 1884, pp. 49-50, 92, 317, 321); J. Polívka, *Drobné Přispěvky Literárněhistorické*, Prague, 1891, p. 102; Solovev, *K legendam ob Iudye predatelye*, Part I, Kharkov, 1898, pp. 78-79, 84 ff.; O. Dähnhardt, *Natursagen*, II, *Sagen zum neuen Testament*, Leipzig, 1909, pp. 236-42, 300; de Cock, *Volkskunde* (Ghent), XXI (1910), 75-76, No. 68 (derived for the most part from Dähnhardt).

[3] Long, "Proverbs: English and Keltic, with their Eastern Relations," *Folk-Lore Record*, III (1880), 1, p. 57. V. S. Lean (*Collectanea*, IV, 22) also cites this saying and remarks, "This was adapted by Dr. Johnson to the bare Brighton downs."

began to tremble in the breeze when Judas hanged himself on one of them.[4]

Before examining the folk-traditions about the tree, let us see what the pilgrims to Jerusalem have reported in the way of local gossip and old wives' tales.[5] Antoninus of Piacenza was shown a fig at the city-gate as he came from Gethsemane: "In dextra parte portae est olivetum; ibi est ficulnea, in qua Iudas se suspendit, cuius talea stat munita petris."[6] This was about 570 A. D. Just about a century later Arculfus also saw a fig of which the same story was told,[7] and Sir John Mandeville, in the fourteenth, an elder. Georg Pfentzing, a worthy patrician of Nuremberg, who visited the Holy Land in 1436 and 1440 and combined the descriptions of his two journeys into a single account, was shown the house of Judas

[4] But this explanation of the quivering of the leaves is, even in Russia, usually restricted to the aspen; see de Gubernatis, I, 143 and Dähnhardt, II, 239.

[5] Although it is not immediately concerned with the *tree* on which Judas hanged himself, I venture to draw attention to another cycle of place-legends which spring from a different root. A French itinerary of the Holy Land declares that as early as 1228 there was a street in Jerusalem called Rue de l'Arc Judas because of the report that Judas had there hanged himself to an arch of stone; see Ernoul, "La Citez de Iherusalem," in Michelant and Raynaud, *Itinéraire à Jerusalem* (*Publ. de la soc. de l'Orient lat., sér. géog.*, III), Geneva, 1882, p. 43. This tradition is repeated in 1261 by the anonymous continuator of Guillaume de Tyr's guide-book; see *ibid.*, p. 156. This street-name implies, therefore, the existence of a tradition counter to the familiar one that the traitor chose a tree and obviously suggests comparison wtih Papias's narrative of his death in a sunken road.

[6] *Antonini Placentini Itinerarium*, ed. J. Gildemeister, Berlin, 1889, p. 13, § 17. In the basilica of St. Mary he saw the very chain: "Vidimus et in uno angulo tenebroso catenam ferream qua se laquearit infelix Iudas," cf. p. 20, § 27.

[7] Palestine Pilgrims' Text Soc., No. X, London, 1889, *The Pilgrimage of Arculfus in the Holy Land* [by St. Adamnan of Hy], p. 19, ch. xviii (with a reference to Bord. Pil., p. 24), see also M. S. L., 88, 790 (*Adamneni De Locis Sanctis*, caput XVIII), which repeats Arculfus. The passage may also be found in Tobler and Molinier, *Itinera Hierosolymitana et Descriptiones Terrae Sanctae*, Genevae, 1879, I, 159: "Ibidem et grandis hodie adhuc monstratum ficus, de cuius, ut fertur, vertice inlaqueatus pependit Iudas, ut Iuvencus, presbyter versificus, cecinit." The same in different words may be found in *Arculfi Relatio Alter*, in Tobler and Molinier, p. 204. Bede copies from Arculfus in his *De Locis Sanctis*, see *ibid.*, p. 221, ch. VI; Solovev, p. 84, n. 2; Hofmann, *Leben Jesu*, p. 333; Pokrovskiï, *Evangelie*, p. 310.

in the valley of Siloam[8] and not far off the tree on which Judas died. "It bears leaves," he adds, without committing himself to a botanical identification.[9] Another German traveller, four years later (1444), saw the tree on a hill near the Mount of Olives, but he, too, fails to record its species.[10] By 1482, however, the tree had disappeared, and was not soon restored to the cicerone's list of sights. For about this year Brother Paul Walter, who sought eagerly such local traditions, found the remains of Judas's house, where (he was told) the Jews did homage and where certain Christians held an annual festival—"laudantes deum non Iudam"!—and was shown the place near by on which the fatal tree had stood.[11] A little later, in 1491, Dietrich von Schachten saw from the Mount of Olives the house of Judas in the vale of Joasaphat, where also, he avers, is the spot on which Judas hanged himself out of despair.[12] Peter Fassbender, citizen of Coblenz, passed through the valley of Siloam the following year (1492), and, looking to the left, saw on the mountain-side the scene of the suicide—but the tree is not mentioned.[13] A merchant of Breslau, Peter Rindfleisch, rode over the crest of Mount Sion on his way to Bethany and saw the spot, not a stone's

[8] R. Röhricht, *Deutsche Pilgerreisen nach dem heiligen Lande*, Berlin, 1880, p. 88.
[9] *Ibid.*, p. 78.
[10] Birlinger, "Ein Pilgerbüchlein: Reise nach Jerusalem von 1444," *Arch. f. d. Studium d. neueren Sprachen*, XL (1867), 317.
[11] M. Sollwerck, *Fratris Pauli Waltheri Guglinensis Itinerarium in Terram Sanctam* (Stuttgart Lit. Ver., CXCII), Stuttgart, 1892, pp. 182-83: "Locum, ubi erat domus Jude Scariothis, qui tradidit Ihesum Judeis et postea ibidem se suspendit. Iste locus non visitatur ut sanctus sed sibi in despectum; et dicunt aliqui, quod Judei honorant locum; et etiam dicunt, quod nonnulli Christiani de nationibus in Iherusalem faciunt annuatim festum de Juda, laudentes deum non Judam," and p. 274: "Judas videns, quod Ihesus damnatus esset . . . laqueo se suspendit. Et presumitur, quod ivit ad domum suam, quia erat prope in latere montis Oliveti ad australem partem, ubi hodie apparet vestigium sue habitationis. Et hanc habitationem fecit depingere sancta Helena in memoriam illius proditoris. Et iuxta illum locum ostenditur locus, ubi stetit arbor, in qua se suspendit."
[12] Röhricht, p. 199.
[13] *Ibid.*, p. 274.

throw from the road, but apparently no tree.[14] Nor did a member of the patrician Rieter family of Nuremberg find there the tree on his visit to the Holy Land about the middle of the sixteenth century.[15]

Turning now to the legends current outside of Palestine, we shall find that the choice of the tree for Judas's gibbet is determined by various influences. Biblical exegesis is clearly visible; and the various attempts to harmonize the two canonical accounts of Judas's end appear repeatedly in the traditions, even in those current only a generation ago. The first choice seems to have been the fig tree.[16] Then other trees were substituted, perhaps because of earlier heathen customs or superstitions, whereby one evil association was replaced by another. Such, for example, is clearly the reason for the appearance of the elder, the willow, and the aspen in this connexion. But in many instances it remains difficult or impossible to see why a particular tree was selected. The explanations which the narrators themselves give do not aid us, for they are obviously whimsical or, so to say, *ad hoc*.

As I have said, the oldest traditions declare that Judas hanged himself on a fig tree (*Ficus carica*).[17] Juvencus, a

[14] *Ibid.*, p. 327. Brother Felix Faber was invited on the occasion of his visit to the Holy Land at the end of the fifteenth century to see the spot, but he spiritedly refused to go out of his way, cf. C. D. Hassler, *Fratris Felicis Fabri Evagatorium*, I (Stutt. Lit. Ver., II [1843]), 421.

[15] Röhricht and Meisner, *Das Reisebuch der Familie Rieter* (Stuttgart Lit. Ver., CLXVIII), 1884, p. 78.

[16] This was the very wild fig tree which Christ cursed, says Folkard (p. 49), who derives his information from de Gubernatis, I, 193. See also Dähnhardt, II, 237. Definite references to places where this identification, which is quite in the spirit of the older exegesis, may be found seem, however, to be lacking. Cf. Schwartz, *Zs. f. neutestamentliche Wiss.*, V (1904).

[17] The queer idea that this fig was the "tree of the knowledge of good and evil" in the Garden of Eden, maintained by Gronovius, is a curiosity of Biblical exegesis which parallels its identification with the wild fig cursed by Christ. It cannot, of course, be quoted as an example of popular legend. See Reinsch in his edition of Juvencus (Francoforti et Lipsiae, 1710, p. 425): "Sunt, qui ficum putent pomum illud, quo Adam transgressus est edictum divinum Judam suspendio periisse, Jac. Gronovius in peculari dissertatione a. 1683 edita, contra Heinsium, Pricatum et Lightfoot evincere conatur." "Pricatum" appears to be John Price (ca. 1600-1676), an Episcopalian turned Romanist; see McClintock and Strong.

Spanish writer of the fourth century, who composed a narrative poem on the Gospels entitled *Historia Evangelica*, describes the suicide as follows:

> Proditor at Judas, postquam se talia cernit,
> Accepto sceleris pretio, signasse furentem
> Infelix aegris damnans sua gesta quaerentis,
> Projecit templo tum detestans argentum
> Exorsusque suas laqueo sibi sumere poenas
> Informem rapuit ficus de vertice mortem.[18]

The Virgilian reminiscences [19] in the passage are pointed out by Reinsch, who believes, moreover, that the last line is not to be understood literally, in spite of the confirmation afforded by Bede, since the poet is using the name of the species for the name of the thing.[20] Bede, we have seen, derives his information from Arculf. Mico (fl. 825-833), the author of the Carolingian *De Cena Domini*, shows in that poem that the notion about the fig had reached Germany by the ninth century:

> Post malesanus enim ficu se sustulit alta
> Faucibus adnexis suasus ab hoste truci.
> Sic planus atque fugax istam finivit amaram.[21]

---

[18] Lib. IV, vv. 627-32 (Migne, Patr. lat., XIX, 31; ed. J. Huemer, Corpus Script. Eccles. Lat., XXIV, Prague, 1881, p. 138).

[19] These are found in the penultimate line of the quotation, which is compared to
> subit ira cadentem
> ulcisci patriam et sceleratas sumere poenas. — Aen. II. 575-76.

And the last line may have been suggested by
> Et nodum informis leti trabe nectit ab alta. — Aen. XII. 603.

Another editor of Juvencus (Faustinus Arevalus, Rome, 1792, p. 373) recalls that St. Leo uses in referring to Judas's death a phrase which may have been derived from the poet: "Informis lethi suspendium distulisses" (Sermo 52 sive 3, de Passione, cap. III).

[20] The following authorities are cited in support of his contention: Ger. Jo. Vossius in *Harmon.*, p. 213; Vossius, *Conf. Sixtum Senensum in Bibliotheca S*, p. 510; Is. Casauboni, *Exercitt. ad Baron.*, LXIX and LXX, p. 529 et seq. The first appears to be G. N. Vossius, *Opera*, VI, *Tractatus Theologici*, Amstelodami, MDCCI, p. 170 (Lib. II, cap. iii, § 29), but the others I do not find.

[21] Monumenta Germaniae Historiae, Poetae aevi Carolini, III, ed. L. Traube, Berlin, 1896, p. 303.

Fray Diego de Hojeda, a Spanish poet whose works were published at Seville in 1611, repeats this tradition in his versified life of Christ:

> A un tronco de higuera levantado
> Se subió, y el espiritu invisible
> Le siguió par darle ayuda en ello,
> Y echóse una gran soga al triste cuello.[22]

The seventeenth century commentator and historian Baronius follows the authority of Juvencus and Bede, defending his opinion by pointing out that the fig of Romulus and Remus lasted through many centuries down to the time of Tacitus and consequently the fig of Judas could similarly have endured to the days of Bede.[23]

The same tradition is still known along the shores of the Mediterranean and in the south of Europe. In Portugal it explains why the fig apparently bears fruit without having blossomed, a prodigy remarked by Aristotle.[24] The Sicilians believe that the fig tree has not borne a flower since Judas's death on it. The Greeks say that the tree bent down with the weight of His body and has since remained bowed; only when Christ ascended into Heaven could Judas die.[25] (This idea that the traitor's death was delayed until after the Ascension is traceable to exegetical speculation on the sequence of events after the Crucifixion and will be met with again in the following pages). So far as Europe north of the Alps is concerned it seems reasonably clear that the choice of the fig tree as Judas's gallows was solely a learned tradition, imported from

[22] *La Christiada*, Libro VII (*Biblioteca de Autores Españoles*, XVII [Madrid, 1866], 455).

[23] *Annales ann. Christi* 34, num. 76.

[24] See B. Laufer, *Sino-Iranica: Chinese Contributions to the History of Civilization* (Field Museum of Nat. Hist., Pub. 201, Chicago, 1919), p. 411.

[25] Leite da Vasconcellos, *Tradições populares de Portugal*, Porto, 1882, pp. 108 f., cf. Sébillot, *Rev. des trad. pop.*, IV (1889), 410; Pitre, "Appunti di botanica popolara siciliana," *Rivista Europea*, 1875, ii, 441, and his *Usi e costume, credenze e pregiudizi del popolo siciliano*, III (Bib. delle trad. pop. sic., XVI, Palermo, 1889), p. 244; de Gubernatis, II, 139; N. G. Polites, Μέλεται περὶ τοῦ βίου καὶ τῆς γλώσσης τοῦ ἑλληνικοῦ λαοῦ, Athens, 1904, No. 183; *Cesta do zeme svate*, I, 143 (cited by Polívka, p. 102, n. 1).

the South where the fig was native, or brought into the account by commentators. In Bohemia, for example, it is found in a vernacular description of the Holy Land, but is presumably not current there among the folk. Only in countries where the fig is a familiar tree is the belief still circulated by the folk and its association with the traitor even in such lands is, as we shall see, not undisputed.

An easy adaption of the fig tradition to more northerly climes, however, is the replacing of the Oriental fig by the closely related sycamore, the so-called "European fig" (*Ficus sycomorus*). In the sixteenth century Adrichomius, a Dutch traveller to the Holy Land, was shown a sycamore, which was declared to have been Judas's gallows. The tree was, he says, still to be seen in a grove on the western slope of Mount Sion.[26] Faustinus Arevalus also seems to be acquainted with this little known tradition, for he says distinguishing the sycamore from the fig: "Nonnulli tradiderunt Judam se ex sambuco suspendisse, alii ex sycomoro, plerique ex ficu."

According to a somewhat younger tradition, which is mentioned in the passage just quoted, Judas is also said to have hanged himself on an elder (*Sambucus nigra*), wherefore it became pithy, or, according to other accounts, its berries became bitter. It seems likely that the intimate connection of the elder with heathen practices — a connection which is apparent from the number and the nature of the superstitions which still cling to this tree — was the reason for its selection as the instrument of the betrayer's suicide, for by attaching the name of Judas to the tree pious teachers might easily

[26] *In theatro terrae sanctae*, p. 175; cf. Cristiano Adricomio, *Gerusalemme e suoi Dindorni ai Tempi di Gesù Cristo* (tr. Fr. Baldelli), Genova, 1882, p. 110, No. 234. The Baldelli translation was first published at Florence in 1594. There are cited in the margin: "Broc. itin. 6b; Sal. tom. 8. cap. 5," which I have not seen. The first I take to be: *Diligentissima descrizione della citta di Gerusalemme dei luogi di Terra Sancta fatta da Brocardo monaco* . . . Basel, 1583 or *Disegno e descrizione di Gerusalemme e della Terra di Promessone fatti con acutissima diligenza* per Bonaventura Brocardo Bernaito, Paris, 1544; the second is *Descrizione del viaggio di Gerusalemme e di Terra Santa* . . . da Bartolomeo da Saligniacio, Lione, 1522.

rouse a repugnance to it in the minds of new converts.[27] The same end — the avoidance of the elder — was also obtained by the exactly opposite means, i. e., its identification with the wood of the Cross.

The tradition connecting Judas with the elder is most widely disseminated in England, France, and Germany. In England it occurs as early as the fourteenth century and has persisted down to the present in both folk-lore and literature. The author of the *Vision of Piers Plowman* wrote

> Judas he iaped - with Iuwen siluer.
> And sithen on an eller - honged hym after.[28]

A majority of the manuscripts of the *Northern Passion*, which dates from the beginning of the fourteenth century, also say that the tree was an elder.[29] At least four Elizabethan dramatists, Marlowe, Shakespeare, Ben Jonson, and Thomas Heywood, allude to the tradition.[30] An Elizabethan herbal, moreover, declares that Judas committed suicide on the "Arbor Judae and not the elder" — which implies that some held the contrary opinion.[31] Sir Thomas Browne mentions the elder as well as the Arbor Judae and the fig.[32] The tradi-

---

[27] In J. H. Stone's *England's Riviera*, p. 457 occurs this fantastic suggestion: "As is well known, the elder is devoid of heartwood, but is full of pith, so perhaps the legend of Judas's association with the tree arose from the fact that the elder may be called the heartless wood. It was a heartless deed to betray so good a Master." — On the extremely interesting folk-beliefs concerning the elder see Sagittarius, *Notes and Queries*, 12th Ser., VI, 259-60, and the references there given.

[28] A text, Passus I, 65; B text, Passus I, 67; C text, Passus II, 63. Cf. Skeat's ed., Oxford, 1886, I, 26-27 and notes, II, 23.

[29] Ed. Miss F. A. Foster, E. E. T. S., 145, London, 1913, I, 86-87. So the oldest MSS; two late MSS say simply "on a tre."

[30] *Jew of Malta*, IV (at end; ed. A. Dyce, London, 1850, II, 173); *Love's Labour's Lost*, V, ii, 610 (Variorum Shakespeare, p. 288), cf. Tschischwitz, *Nachklänge germanischer Mythen in den Werken Shakespeares*, pp. 41 ff.; *Every Man Out of His Humour*, IV, iv, cf. Gifford, *Works of Ben Jonson*, II (London, 1875), 141 and the parallel from Nixon, *Strange Footpost*); *Woman Killed with Kindness*, IV, v.

[31] Gerarde, *The Herball Historie of Plantes* (ed. Johnson, 1633), p. 1428, and quoted by Furness, Variorum Shakespeare and Brand, *Popular Antiquities* (ed. Hazlitt), III (1870), 244, n. 2. The "Arbor Judae" is the wild carob; on its association with Judas see below.

[32] *Works* (ed. Sayle), I, 304 (*Pseudodoxia Epidemica*, II, vii).

tion appears a little later in the jingling rhymes of Richard Flecknoe's *Diarium:*

> How Alder-stick in pocket carried,
> By Horseman who on highway feared
> His Breech should nere be galled or wearied,
> Although he rid on trotting Horse,
> Or Crow, or Cowl-staff which was worse,
> It had, he aid, such vertuous force
> Where Vertue oft from Judas came
> (Who hang'd himself upon the same;
> For which, in sooth, he was to blame).[33]

It is, moreover, still current among the folk.[34] In the North Riding of Yorkshire "to be crowned with elder is noted as a mark of extreme degradation because Judas is said to have hung himself on an elder-tree."[25] The Manx, too, know the story, but the elder is no less respected for its curative powers:

> The Elder tree, or the Tramnan, was vulgarly supposed to have been the tree upon which Judas Iscariot hanged himself, and it was possibly on this account that great reliance was formerly placed in its sanative and mystical virtues. It was used as a charm for protecting houses and gardens from the influence of sorcery and witchcraft, and, even at the present time, an Elder tree may be observed growing by almost every cottage in the Island. Its leaves like those of the Cuirn (Thorn tree) were picked on May eve and affixed to doors and windows to protect the house from witchcraft.[36]

In Leitrim, Waterford, and the south of Ireland, also, the

---

[33] Ed. 1656, p. 65 (quoted in Brand-Hazlitt, III, 244), see also W. W. Seymour, *Cross in Tradition, History, and Art,* p. 95.

[34] Miss G. F. Jackson, *Shropshire Word-Book,* s.v. Ellern. Cf. Miss C. S. Burne, *Shropshire Folklore,* pp. 243-44. Miss Burne suggests that the alder may really be meant, but this is unlikely since the elder (*Sambucus*) is so often mentioned in this connection, and the alder rarely, if ever, is.— Leicester: M. A. B., *Notes and Queries,* 8th Ser., VIII, 427 (30 Nov., 1895); Kent: J. Britten and R. Holland, *Dictionary of English Plant Names* (Eng. Dial. Soc., Ser. C, IX), London, 1878, p. 547.

[35] Mrs. Gutch, *Folklore of the North Riding* (Publ. Folklore Soc., XLV, London, 1901), p. 62, citing F. K. Robinson, *A Glossary of Words Used in the Neighborhood of Whitby,* Eng. Dial. Soc., 1876, p. 29.

[36] A. W. Moore, *Folk-lore of the Isle of Man,* Douglas, 1891, p. 152 and quoted in *Notes and Queries,* 10th Ser., viii, 213 (Sept., 1907).

elder or "bore" tree suffers under this ignominious accusation, and the truth of the slander is demonstrated by the "ugly smell" of the leaves and the fact that the fruit has degenerated from its former size and flavor until it is now quite worthless.[37]

Outside of the British Isles the identification of Judas's gibbet with the elder is equally common. The oldest allusion is perhaps that in a *Passion* which Emile Roy calls the *Passion des Jongleurs*, dating from the end of the twelfth or the beginning of the thirteenth century. Jean d'Outremeuse, who employed for his *Chronique* a more complete manuscript than that published by Chabaneau, proses the phrase: "Apres prist Judas sa chinture et le loiat en son coul, et se soy pendit a une arbre que ons nom sahus." In the *Passion de Semur*, which belongs probably to the first third of the fifteenth century, Judas cries twice in his agony, "Hee! diable, or me conseille." Then *Mors Inferni* advises him to hang himself, and *Clamator Inferni* says:

> Judas, voirement cy ferons,
> Or tost passe pour ton peut heur . . .
> Va, cy te pent a ce cehur,
> Car tu nous doit huy l'ame randre.[38]

Almost as old is a passage in Greban's *Mystère de la Passion* (before 1452), where *Desesperance* to Judas's question:

> a quel gibet me pendera je?
> Desesperance, qu'en dis tu?

replies

> Voicy ung viel shur tortu
> qui a des branches largement
> et te soustendra puissament:
> monte sus, et je t'ayderay.[39]

---

[37] "Notes on Irish Folk-Lore," *Folk-Lore*, XXVII (1916), 425.

[38] Ed. Émile Roy in *Le Mystère de la Passion en France*, Dijon and Paris, 1903-4, p. 135. The *Passion des Jongleurs* is analyzed on pp. 27* ff.; see particularly p.31*. Chabaneau's text, cited by Roy, will be found in *Rev. des langues rom.*, XXVIII, 157-258. Cf. Jean d' Outremeuse, *Chronique*, I (1864), 409. Professor George L. Hamilton called my attention to these allusions.

[39] Ed. G. Paris and G. Raynaud, Paris, 1878, p. 287.

The tradition is still current in France: in Haute Bretagne it explains why the elder has lost its former beneficent medical qualities; the scent of its flowers is that of the traitor's body; and to offer any one elder-water is a particularly pointed insult.[40] And in the same département it is believed that the fruit of the elder became so bitter, after Judas had hanged himself on the tree, that it could not be eaten.[41] Furthermore, the folk in northern France (Pas-de-Calais and la Marne) see Judas in the moon, hanging to an elder by his hair or by his feet.[42] The same tradition appears in northern Germany with similar explanations as well.[43] That it has not been reported for the South of Germany is probably accidental. Finally, the whole question would be settled if one could only believe the assertion of Sir John Mandeville who claimed to have seen the tree, an elder, in the early years of the fourteenth century not far from the pool of Siloam.[44] No doubt the frequency of the tradition in western Europe is largely due to the popularity of that collection of travels.

[40] Lucie de V. H., "Traditions de la Haute Bretagne, No. 87, Le sureau maudit," *Rev. des trad. pop.*, XXV (1910), 312.

[41] Sébillot, *Le Folklore de France*, III (Paris, 1906), 369 (from Sébillot, *Rev. des trad. pop.*, IV [1889], 410). His reference to J. B. Andrews, *Rev. des tard. pop.*, IX (1894), 216 seems to be erroneous.

[42] Sébillot, *op. cit.*, I (Paris, 1904), 19 (from a communication of M. Edmont [Saint Pol, Pas-de-Calais] and from Heuilliard, *Rev. des trad. pop.*, XVIII [1903], 375 [la Marne]). There are other traditions to the effect that Judas is seen in the moon, but they do not mention the elder.

[43] Perger, *Deutsche Pflanzensagen*, Stuttgart, 1864, pp. 260-61; R. Pieper, *Volksbotanik*, Gumbinnen, 1897, p. 324; Strackerjan, *Aberglaube und Sagen aus dem Herzogtum Oldenburg*, 2nd ed. by Willoh, Oldenburg, 1909, II, 122, § 354; Bartsch, *Sagen aus Mechlenburg*, I, 524, No. 38.

[44] *Voiage and Travaille*, 1725, p. 112; Bohn ed., p. 175; ed. Halliwell, 1839, p. 93 ("with a quaint woodcut of Judas hanging from a conventional tree, most unlike an elder"). See also G. F. Warner, *The Buke of John Maundeville*, Roxburghe Club, Westminister, 1889, p. 46 (the elder is not mentioned in the English text, but appears in the French) and the notes (p. 183) in which I have been unable to identify Boldensele. Cf. Ceyrep, *Notes and Queries*, 1st Ser., VII, 334 (2 April, 1853); St. Swithin, *ibid.*, 11th Ser., XII, 470 (11 Dec., 1915); Dyce, *Marlowe*, 1850, II, 173. See also J. H. Stone, *England's Riviera*, p. 457, who cites a remark on this passage in the *Travels* from the *Quarterly Rev.*, CXIV (1863), 233 to the effect that this "piece of English folklore had its roots in the old heathenism of the North."

Similar but somewhat less widespread than the others is the belief that Judas chose a willow to die upon; and like them probably influenced by earlier heathen superstitions.[45] With it is combined an obvious reminiscence of the account of Judas's death in Acts 1:18. For example, in Pomerania they say:

> When Judas Iscariot had betrayed our Lord, he hanged himself on a willow, and, falling down, his body burst asunder, and his bowels fell upon the ground. Since then the willow rarely exceeds the height of a man and must bend its twigs to the earth. And like Judas it must scatter its bowels [i. e., pith], since all willows become hollow as they grow old.[46]

Much the same tradition is current in Limburg, Mecklenburg, Bavaria and doubtless other parts of Germany, as well as in Spain. In Portugal it is used to explain the absence of fruit on the willow. In the Tyrol, on the other hand, Judas is said to have selected the grape vine — a manifestly absurd notion due probably to a confusion of the Italian *vite* and the German *wîde* (Weide).[47]

Still another tree which has been associated with the death of Judas, also under the influence of heathen superstitions, is the aspen (*Populus tremula*). This association is predominantly Slavic. In Bohemia it is said that the aspen has trembled since Judas hanged himself on it.[48] In Poland, too,

[45] Dähnhardt, II, 241.

[46] Jahn, *Volkssagen aus Pommern und Rügen*, Stettin, 1886, p. 491, § 609, ii.

[47] Creizenach, *Beiträge*, II (1876), 183; Dähnhardt, II, 240; Boekenoogen, *Volkskunde* (Ghent), XV (1904), 116, No. 38; Bartsch, *Sagen aus Mecklenburg*, I, 524; Handtmann, *Was auf märkischer Heide spriesst*, p. 13 (cf. Dähnhardt, II, 290, n. 1 on the merits of this book); Perger, *Deutsche Pflanzensagen*, p. 312; de Cock, *Volkskunde*, XXI (1910), 75; Leoprechting, *Aus dem Lechrain*, Munich, 1855, p. 99; Crombie, "Some Spanish Superstitions," *Folk-Lore Journal*, I (1883), 295; Leite da Vasconcellos, *Tradiçoes populares de Portugal*, No. 234 f.; Sébillot, *Rev. des trad. pop.*, IV (1889), 410.

[48] Kögler, "Aus Grossmutters Munde," *Mitt. des nordböhm. Exkursionsklubs*, XX (1897), 74. Cf. also Pr. Sobotka, *Rostlinstvo*, pp. 112-23 (cited by Polívka, p. 102, n.1).

As examples of these non-Christian beliefs may be mentioned the warning, frequent in Poland, against standing under an aspen in a thunder-storm, for the lightning is most likely to strike there, and the use of aspen twigs as protection

the leaves of the aspen shake in recollection of the event.⁴⁹ In southern Russia, where the tradition seems to be the most widely current, it explains why the leaves of the aspen quiver with the slightest breeze and why they assume a brilliant red hue, the color of blood, in the autumn.⁵⁰ Ukrainians in the government of Kharkov say that when Judas hanged himself on an aspen the tree bowed its branches so that the traitor's feet touched the ground and he could not die. The tree did this lest Judas die before the Saviour, and, arriving in Hell before Him, be freed in the Harrowing of Hell. Judas hung alive on the lowered branch until his Master had returned to earth, when the tree straightened itself, tightening the cord about his neck so that he died.⁵¹ In the adjoining governments of Podalia, Poltava, Kiev, and Chernigov the quivering of the aspen's leaves is declared to be due to its recollection of the time when Judas hung suspended from its limbs.⁵² A White Russian tale relates that, when Judas hanged himself to an aspen, Christ bent it down to the ground and commanded

against vampires and witches (Kopernicki as cited in *Globus*, XXXV [1879], 270-71). The connection with Judas is apparent in the phrases "buty tobi na osysci" (may you be on an aspen) and "ego treba poisyty na osynu, yak parsivu" (he must be hanged on an aspen like a dirty dog). Another tradition, moreover, traducing the fair name of the aspen, explains that the tree trembles because it revealed Christ to the Jews when He had concealed Himself beneath its branches.

⁴⁹ Siarkowski, "Podania i legendy o zwiérzetach, drzwach i roslinach," *Zbiór wiadomosci do antropologii Krajowej* (Cracow), VII (1883), (118), No. 39.

⁵⁰ L. N., *Etnograficeskoye Obozreniye*, XIII-XIV (Moscow, 1892), 97.

⁵¹ Solovev, p. 78. A similar legend in Greek about the fig-tree has already been noted. R. W. Hackwood (*Notes and Queries*, 2nd Ser., VI, 118 [7 Aug., 1858]) cites an Armenian legend narrating how the Devil kept Judas in limbo until Christ had left Hell, lest the traitor escape his due. This manner of Judas's death is represented on the brass doors of the archiepiscopal church at Beneventano; cf. W. W. Seymour, *The Cross in Tradition*, p. 95 n. These legends seem to rest ultimately on the exegesis of Origen and Theophylact. Theophylact (*ad Matth.*, 27; cf. R. Hoffman, *Leben Jesu*, p. 333) says that the tree on which Judas hanged himself bent down so that he could not die; see also Origen, *In Matth.* tract. 35, *contra Celsum*, II (M. S. G., XI, 836); Solovev, p. 72, and below, p. 000.

⁵² Solovev, p. 78 (Podalia, Poltava, Kiev), p. 85, n. 2 (Chernigov); Efimenko, p. 42; Sumtsov, *Ocerki istorii yuznorusskikh skazaniĭ i pyesn*, p. 102. Folkard (p. 50) mentions the tradition as Ukrainian.

it to tremble day and night without a breeze.⁵³ Certainly this story is nothing more than a modification of the previous one in which the bending arises from the tree's volition; and it is strange to find any suggestion that Christ himself showed a desire to have his betrayer punished — indeed, as we shall see, one folk-tale declares that He wished to pardon the sinner — for the notion of vengefulness is so foreign to His nature that its appearance here is undoubtedly a vagary of popular tradition. Another queer story, said to be current in Lithuania, relates that when Judas fled into the forest to hang himself the trees awoke and would not allow the wretched sinner to approach them. Only the aspen was asleep and, taking advantage of the situation, Judas hanged himself on it. When it awoke and found his body suspended from a branch it was so terrified that it began to tremble — and this trembling is still characteristic of the tree.⁵⁴ The Russian proverb, "There is an accursed tree which trembles without a breath of wind," is said to allude to Judas's suicide,⁵⁵ and throughout Russia similar traditions seem to be associated with the aspen.⁵⁶

A curious tale which mentions the aspen in this connection is related in Wendish Lusatia:

During Christ's wanderings on this earth he came with his disciples to a little house owned by a widow. She was willing to entertain Him, but she was so poor that she could not buy any food. He said, however, that He would buy thirty silver pieces' worth of bread, and asked which one of the disciples would fetch it. Judas volunteered at once and took the money. On his way to the street of the Jews he fell in with a company of Jews who were gambling. They invited Judas to join them; at first he was hesitant, but finally he wagered a part of the money entrusted to him and won. A second

⁵³ Romanov, *Byelorusskiĭ Sbornik*, p. 232; cf. Solovev, p. 85, n. 2.
⁵⁴ R. Pieper, *Volksbotanik*, Gumbinnen, 1897, p. 466 (no authority is cited).
⁵⁵ Folkard, p. 50 (citing Dal's collection of proverbs, Moscow, 1862, but giving neither page nor number).
⁵⁶ Sinval, "Les Russes chez eux," *La Tradition*, IV (1890), 253; de Gubernatis, I, 193; Dähnhardt, II, 239 citing *Etn. Sbornik*, VI, i, 126; *Smolenskiĭ etn. Sbornik*, I (*Zapiski imp. rus. geog. ob.*, XX), I, 245, No. 29.

time he risked the whole sum and won. The third time he lost. The Jews offered to return the thirty silver pieces if he would deliver up his Master, and Judas assented to the proposal. While Christ and His disciples were sitting at supper, He asked, "Which one of you has sold me?" John, Peter, and Judas asked, "Is it I?" To Judas He replied, "Judas, Judas, thou false Judas, thou knowest best." Then Judas rose and rushed out to hang himself. Christ called after him, "Return, O Judas, your sin is forgiven, and your punishment remitted." But Judas did not hear, and ran on until he reached a forest. To the pine he said, "Your wood is too soft, and my sin too heavy; you, pine, cannot bear me." He hanged himself on an aspen and from that moment it has quivered and trembled as it will do until the Day of Judgment.[57]

A Russian tale from the government of Tver declares oddly enough that Judas did *not* hang himself on the aspen:

Judas the traitor knew that Christ would bring out all those who were in Hell. So when he had betrayed his Master, he planned to leave the Garden and keep the money. Then he ran to hang himself in order to reach Hell before Christ. He ran to one tree to hang

[57] Haupt, *Sagenbuch der Lausitz*, p. 193; Dähnhardt, II, 239-40; Dähnhardt, *Naturgeschichtliche Märchen*, I (Vierte vermehrte Auflage, 1912), pp. 77-78, No. 56. See also P. F. Baum, "The English Ballad of Judas Iscariot," *Publ. Mod. Lang. Ass.*, XXXI (1916), 181-89.

The notion emphasized by this story that, if Judas had repented, Christ would have pardoned him, and that perhaps his greater sin was not his treachery but his sinful despair of the mercy of God and his consequent suicide appears in various mediaeval writers. Solovev (pp. 110-11) cites Dulaurier, *Fragments des révélations apocryphes de saint Barthélemy*, Paris, 1835; "Acta Pauli et Andrae," Tischendorf, *Apocalypses apocryphae* (Judas's soul is not set free from Hell, "eo quod iste antequam se suspendisset"); the Russian *Speculum majus* (in a passage reprinted in Appendix IV, pp. 142-43); Schröder, *Sanct Brandan*, p. 114. He quotes from a Middle High German sermon (Leyser, *Predigten*, p. 34): If you despair of God's mercy, "so tuostu als Caym und Judas, die da ewichliche vertuomet sint unt verlorn. wanne hetten sie genade gesucht an gotte, so hetten sie genade an im vunden." See further Lecompte, *Mod. Lang. Notes*, XXXIV (1919), 307; Birlinger, *Alemannia*, VII (1879), 221; *La Vie de Saint Gile* (ed. Paris and Bos, Soc. des anc. textes, 1881), p. 85, vv. 2805 ff.; Büchner, *Judas Ischarioth in der deutschen Dichtung*, Freiburg i. B., 1920, citing Suso, ed. Diepenbrock, 1854, p. 395. Peter Comestor (M. S. L., CXCVIII, 1625) says: "Dicit Hieronymus super CVIII. psal. quia magis offendit Judas Deum, quando se suspendit, quam in hoc quod prodidit"; cf. Miss F. A. Foster, *Northern Passion*, II, 60.

himself to its branches, but it bowed to the ground; and a second one did the same. He ran and ran, but no tree would take him. It meant that our Lord did not wish his suicide but his repentance; Judas had no desire to repent of his crime, but wished only to hang himself so that he might reach Hell as quickly as possible. He realized that haste was necessary. Finally he caught sight of a sunken road, and on the edge of it a tree which was on the point of falling over. Judas hastened to it and the tree fell on him with such violence that his eyes were squeezed out of his forehead. .But he had failed to reach Hell before his Master, who had already freed the souls there. Thus Judas, still bearing his purse, was the first to come to Hell after Christ's visit. Judas slew himself in this manner, and not by hanging himself on an aspen. With his money the village "Skudelbnoye" [The Wretched] was purchased, but in it there prevails even today so disgusting an odor that only snakes can live there.[58]

The association of the aspen with Judas's suicide is but rarely encountered outside of Slavic territory. Napier reports it from the West of Scotland, with the usual explanation that the leaves of the aspen have quivered ever since.[59] Kamp notes its occurrence in the western part of the Danish province of Seeland. Judas hanged himself on an aspen because it was the first tree he met after he had cast the thirty pieces of silver into the temple; since then its leaves tremble with fright.[60]

The Sicilians say that the tamarind (*Tamerix gallica*), which is now a shrub, was once a tree large enough to bear the body of Judas. After his suicide the tree bent down, became

[58] *Zhivaya Starina*, IX (1889), 392, cf. Dähnhardt, II, 300-301. The haste to reach Hell which animates Judas is a reminiscence of the exegesis of Origen and Theophylact (see above, p. 147). I suspect that the narrator was also recalling exegetical endeavors to harmonize the conflicting accounts of Judas's death. It is often explained, for example by Euthymius and Oecumenius, that Judas hanged himself on a tree which stood on the edge of a cliff and that his body, in falling, burst. Observe also that the scene, a sunken road, recalls the narrative of Papias. For a convenient collection of the early exegetical comments on Judas's death see Locard, "La mort de Judas," *Archives d'anthropologie criminelle*, XIX (1904), 421 ff.

[59] J. Napier, *Folk-Lore or Superstitious Beliefs in the West of Scotland*, Paisley, 1879, p. 124.

[60] *Danske Folkeminder* (Dähnhardt, II, 239 gives no page and I have not seen the book).

smaller and smaller, until it was no larger than a bush.⁶¹ From this story comes the phrase "tintu comu la vruca," and the couplet, taken from a song,—

> Chi nun fa ne cinniri ne focu.
> Si' come lu lignu di la vruca.

Moreover, Judas's soul, they say, is condemned to float forever in the air without being able to rise higher or fall lower, stopping whenever it sees a tamarind to watch the struggles of its body reënacted by the soulless corpse swaying to and fro.⁶² It should be remarked that this appalling picture is not original with the Sicilian peasant, but is derived from the *Legenda Aurea*: "In aere etiam interiit, ut qui angelos in coelo et homines in terra offenderat, ab angelorum et hominum regione separaretur et in aere cum daemonibus sociaretur." The ultimate source is a remark of Candidus (c. 822) or of Petrus Comestor.⁶³ In Russia the tradition, which is obviously learned and not popular, has been circulated by the *Beseda Trekh Svyatitelei* (Disputation of Three Saints), a series of questions concerning Bible story derived ultimately from Greek sources.⁶⁴ Some of the Russian versions answer the question, "What is the name of the tree on which Judas hanged himself?" with *mirniki* (tamarind, cf. μυρίκη), as do the Serbian versions.⁶⁵ The question and answer in the Greek, the source, read:

Τὸ δένδρον ὅπου ἀπήγξατο ὁ 'Ιούδας τί ἦν; 'Απok. Μυρίχη (var. μυρίκη).

⁶¹ Pitrè, "Appunti di botanica popolara siciliana," *Rivista Europea*, 1875, II, 441 and his *Usi e costume, credenze e pregiudizi*, III, 227; cf. Dähnhardt, II, 241, and Folkard, pp. 49-50.

⁶² Pitrè, *Fiabe, novelle e racconti popolari siciliani*, Palermo, 1875, I, p. cxxxviii and tr. in Crane, *Italian Popular Tales*, Boston, 1885, p. 195; see also de Gubernatis, I, 194; Dähnhardt, II, 241.

⁶³ See P. F. Baum, "The Mediaeval Legend of Judas Iscariot." *Publ. Mod. Lang. Ass.*, XXXI (1916), 517-18 and n. 29. The author of the *Passional* (ed. Hahn), p. 318, alludes to the notion.

⁶⁴ Cf. Foerster, *Anglia*, XLII (1918), 213; *Zhurnal ministerstva narodnago prosveshtcheniya*, CCCL, 206-21; N. Th. Krasnosiltsev, "K voprosu o gretcheskikh istotchnikakh 'Besedy trekh svyatitelei,'" *Zapiski novorossikago universiteta* (Kiev), XXI, 431.

⁶⁵ See Polívka, p. 102 and n. 1; Solovev, p. 85, n. 5. The former cites:

One tree has the dubious honor of owing its popular name to its association with Judas: the wild carob or false St. John's Bread (*Cercis siliquastrum*), which is widely known as the Judas tree (arbre de Judas [Judée], Judasbaum, Judasboom, arvulu di Giuda [Giudea]).[66] These names are probably misunderstandings of *arbor Judae* (tree of Judæa) and indicate the foreign origin of the tree as well as of the tradition. The tree is not often the subject of tales among the folk except in the South of Europe where it is indigenous.[67] The *Encyclopedia Britannica* remarks that the wild carob is "frequently figured by the older herbalists"— implying that it was an unfamiliar tree — and mentions particularly a woodcut by Castor Durante in which Judas is depicted as hanging from its branches. Sir Thomas Browne refers to the Judas tree, meaning no doubt the wild carob, in the *Pseudodoxia Epidemica*, VII, i: "Yet can we not infer . . . the Arbor Judae to be the same which supplied the gibbet unto Judas."[68] The employment of the Latin name may mean that the tradition was not yet naturalized in England. Be that as it may, the belief is now current in Hampshire.[69] In the

Tikhonravov, *Pomyatniki otretch. russkoĭ lit.*, II, 430; *Arkiv za povjest. jugosl.*, IX, 107; Safarik, *Rukopisi srbski*, p. 12. But these I have been unable to find.

[66] *Enc. Brit.*, 11th ed., XV, 536, *s.v.* Judas tree; the *Century Dictionary* remarks (*s.v.*) that this was "originally" the Judas tree, but why this is so is not apparent; A. S. Palmer, *Folk-Etymology*, London, 1882, *s.v.* (but the term is not necessarily Spanish); Folkard (pp. 49-50) cites Gerarde's *Herball Historie* (1633), which has been quoted above; German: Frisch, *Teutsch-lateinisches Wörterbuch*, I, 493, *s.v.* Judasbaum: "Eine art des wilden Johannisbeerbaums"; Pritzel-Jessen, *Die deutschen Volksnamen der Pflanzen*, p. 88; Solovev, p. 84; Dähnhardt, II, 241; Dutch: Van Wijk, *A Dictionary of Plant Names*, The Hague, 1912-16, *s.v.* Judasboom; French: de Gubernatis, I, 193, II, 50; Sicilian: Pitrè, "Appunti di botanica popolara siciliana," *Rivista Europea*, 1875, II, 441. The Spaniards call the tree "arbol de amor," which suggests another legend. A. Lyttkens, *Svenska växtnamn*, 1904-15, contains nothing of interest here. There is an apparently significant essay in E. Lemke, *Asphodelos und anderes aus Natur und Volkskunde*, I (Allenstein, 1914).

[67] See, e.g., Pitrè, *Usi e costume, credenze e pregiudizi del popolo siciliano*, III, 295.

[68] *Works* (ed. Sayle), London, 1907, III, 2.

[69] *Hampshire Independent*, 27 June, 1891, reprinted in *Hampshire Antiquary and Naturalist*, II (1891), 60. R. C. A. Prior (*The Popular Names of British*

United States, too, the notion has been adopted by the folk with the necessary transference to the local species, the red bud (*Cercis canadensis*), and by way of proof is adduced the fact that the tree has blushed ever since, — an allusion to the abundance of purplish pink flowers which appear before the leaves.[70]

Possibly to be associated with this tradition about the wild carob or false St. John's bread is a similar one concerning the true St. John's bread (*Ceratonia siliqua*) to which Pulci alludes in the *Morgante Maggiore*. The traitor Ganelon plans the ambush in the pass of Roncesvalles under the shade of a tree which belonged to the same species as the one on which Judas hanged himself:

> Fra disopra alla fonte un carrubbio,
> L'arbor, si dice, ove s'impiccò Giuda.[71]

A half-dozen other trees have been identified with Judas's gibbet, but all more or less casually. In the Russian catechetical dialogue just mentioned, the *Disputation of Three Saints*, the question as to the tree Judas chose is occasionally answered by naming the oak (*Quercus*).[72] And this tradition recurs in some manuscripts of the *Strasti Gospodni* (Passion of our Lord). Although it not exclusively restricted to Russia or countries accepting the Greek confession, it seems to have

Plants[2], 1870, p. 124) is familiar with it, see Britten and Holland, *Dictionary of English Plant Names* (Eng. Dial. Soc., Sec. C, IX, London, 1878), p. 281. Cf. *Notes and Queries*, 2nd Ser., IX, 433 (2 June, 1860) for some remarks on the hardiness of the tree in the English climate.

[70] From an oral source (Missouri). See also J. R. Bartlett, *Dictionary of Americanisms*[4], Boston, 1896, p. 517; J. S. Farmer, *Americanisms Old and New*, London, 1889, p. 327.

[71] Canto XXV, st. 77 (ed. Volpi, III [1904], 201), cf. Dyce, *Marlowe*, II, 173 and St. Swithin, *Notes and Queries*, 11th Ser., XII, 470. C. Curto (*Le tradizioni popolari nel "Morgante" di Luigi Pulci*, Casal, 1918) does not mention it. See also E. C. Brewer, *Reader's Handbook*, s.v. Judas tree, where it is said that the St. John's Bread was called Arbor Judae, which in turn was misinterpreted as "Judas tree." He is thinking of the wild carob. See also J. Holmboe, "Plantenavnet buxhorn [*Ceratonia siliqua*] i 'Postola sögur'," *Maal og Minne*, 1917, 168.

[72] A. N. Pypin, *Pomyatniki star. russ. lit.*, III, 172 (cited by Polívka, p. 102, n. 1).

soon died out in western Europe. In an Italian painting of the fifth century Judas is represented as hanging from the branch of an oak.[73] The same tradition appears on an ivory in the British Museum, which Garrucci dates in the fifth century and Westwood, between the fifth and the eighth centuries.[74]

The appropriation of certain other trees for this purpose has in each case a very limited currency. Folkard names the dog rose (*Rosa canina*) or eglantine, whose berries are to this day called "Judasbeeren";[75] but he does not make it clear that the two names refer to the same plant nor does he cite his authority. He presumably found the tradition in Perger,[76] who records the belief in Angeln (Schleswig), that since Judas's death the thorns of the eglantine have been turned downwards. Dähnhardt mentions a few more trees. In Malta tradition asserts that Judas hanged himself on the juniper (*Juniperus*), which at that time bore fine fruit. Since then the fruit has turned dark and has shrunk, so that the berries appear as they do today. The Styrians say that the traitor died on a birch (*Betula*).[77] The Maltese also relate the following legend about the poplar:

> When Judas had betrayed our Lord, he sought for a tree on which to hang himself. He was in great despair. At last he caught sight of a poplar covered with fruit. He hanged himself on it and at once the fruit and the dark bark of the tree fell off. Since that time the poplar bears no fruit, and one says of a man who is miserly and good-

[73] Cf. Garrucci, *Storia della arte christiana*, V, Tav. 444 (cited by Solovev, p. 89, n. 1). Solovev devotes a short chapter (pp. 89-94) to "Representations of the Death of Judas." It is not my intention to enter into a discussion of Judas in art, on which see Wilhelm Porte, *Judas Iscariot in der bildenden Kunst*, Jena Diss., Berlin, 1883.

[74] Garrucci, VI, Tav. 446, 2; Westwood, *Fictile Ivories*, London, 1873, p. 53.

[75] Pp. 49, 317.

[76] *Deutsche Pflanzensagen*, p. 236.

[77] Dähnhardt, II, 241 (from Baumgarten, "Aus der volksmässigen Ueberlieferung der Heimat," *Jahresber. d. Mus. zu Linz*, XXIX (1863), Linz, 1864, I, 128). See also Polívka, p. 102, n. 1 (citing his "Opisi," *Starin* (Agram), XXI, p. 25 of the reprint).

for nothing, "He is like the poplar; no one has eaten or tasted anything of it (him) since the days of Judas."[78]

Closely analogous is the German story told along the northern coast to the effect that Judas chose a black poplar (*Populus nigra*), and that his restless spirit still whimpers in its branches so that its leaves quiver.[79]

Thus the lacuna in the Biblical account is more than filled. In the selection of the tree the folk pay, as usual, little or no attention to possibility or plausibility: the elder, the aspen, the oak, or the willow could hardly have been available to Judas for his purpose. The force determining the choice is rather a desire to explain some characteristic of the tree. Typical are the explanations of the tamarind's dwindling into a shrub, of the willow's pith, of the elder's foul odor, and of the pink color of the red bud's blossoms. Such ætiological stories, moreover, may spring up at any time about any tree and bear in themselves no evidence of age. Other stories are told as a result of a hostility or dislike which the folk felt or had been taught to feel toward a particular tree. In these instances it is quite clear that the appearance of the tree in the story of Judas has some connection with a not wholly forgotten pagan life. The elder, the aspen, and the willow were once, as the superstitions still clinging to them show, important in pre-Christian belief and ritual. The sacred things of the older religion were in time associated with objects accursed by the new: pagan gods became devils and demons under the Christian dispensation, and a like change led to a repugnance for beliefs and practices of heathendom: the eating of horseflesh was proscribed by Christian missionaries and was soon frowned upon by the folk. Similarly and probably without much deliberate effort on the part of ecclesiastics the

[78] Dähnhardt, II, 238-39 (from an oral source).
[79] *Ibid.*, II, 240 (from Handtmann, *Was auf märkischer Heide spriesst.* p. 12. On the caution with which material from this book [Handtmann] should be used see Dähnhardt, II, 290, n. l.). R. Pieper (*Volksbotanik*, Gumbinnen, 1897, pp. 468 ff.) copies from Handtmann. Classen (*Die Pflanzewelt in Natur, Geist und Leben*, 1897, I, 176) also mentions the notion.

elder and the aspen came into disrepute, and then it was natural to associate them with the traitor Judas. Like will to like. Thus the present connection with Judas is used to explain a modern aversion to trees which were once venerated. Still other trees have fallen under this disgrace because they happened to belong to species which had representatives in Palestine, and inasmuch as the actual tree which Judas could have chosen was not at hand, the popular mind seized upon its nearest kin. In this way the European fig replaced or became a substitute for the fig, the red bud for the wild carob. A somewhat similar exchange causes, along the Baltic, the poplars to bear the stigma instead of the aspen.

As we have seen, some of these stories cannot be dated, and others spring from very ancient roots. In a few cases very curious points of contact with mediaeval Biblical exegesis have been noted. Perhaps no subject would on first thought be so unlikely to influence popular tradition as the speculations of Biblical critics and their elaborate and artificial interpretations and comparisons of the New and the Old Testaments or, having found its way to the folk, to linger on in legends. Yet there is unmistakable evidence of the persistence of just such material. Reminiscences of Biblical story, e. g., the bursting of Judas's body, are not surprising, and the suggestion, concerning his death, borrowed from the *Legenda Aurea*, might also be expected. But it is interesting to find the exegetical and harmonizing efforts of the early Fathers, from Papias down, reflected in popular story, and to observe that some of these have had a rather wide circulation among the folk. — But of such varied materials is the fabric of folklore woven.

THE BURNING OF JUDAS

ARCHER TAYLOR

Associate Professor of German

In many countries the fires which are lit at the coming of Spring are associated with Easter and with Judas.[1] Sir J. G. Frazer and others have made it clear that these fires are not Christian in origin, but are the remnants of pagan rites, now veiled under a Christian covering. Their original significance is still a disputed question. Frazer, following Westermarck, is now inclined to believe that they were first conceived as purificatory. An older explanation, which is due to Mannhardt, sees in them a ceremony "intended, on the principle of imitative magic, to ensure a needful supply of sunshine for men, animals, and plants by kindling fires which mimic on earth the great source of light and heat in the sky."[2] It is not necessary here to choose between these hypotheses. In whatever way the custom of a ceremonial fire at certain seasons of the year may have arisen, the Church found the folk firmly attached to it and, rather than risk a conflict over the question of its abolition, the missionaries concealed its true nature under the cloak of a Christian name or holy day. The midwinter fires became a Christian festival and those

[1] I have included in what follows references to customs of beating or reviling Judas as well as to fires in which his effigy is burned. Today at least the folk conceive the beating and the burning in much the same sense, and I am interested in the subject primarily in its relation to the traitor. The material as it touches Judas has not been separately gathered, see e.g., U. Jahn, *Die deutschen Opfergebräuche*, p. 131, n. 1. Many references I owe to the kindness of Professor Hugo Hepding of Giessen.

[2] Frazer, *Golden Bough*,[3] VII, i, 329. The two parts of vol. VII, *Balder the Beautiful*, deal at length with these ceremonial fires. See also W. Mannhardt, *Wald- und Feldkulte*, I, 502 ff. and U. Jahn, *Die deutschen Opfergebräuche* (Germanist. Abh. 3), pp. 121 ff.

at other seasons of the year were associated with an appropriate saint's day. Some which were never completely adapted in this fashion, for example the Celtic Beltaine, celebrated in May, have always remained under a cloud.

The fires which in the Christian interpretation are a punishment of Judas have in spite of their actual origin, had a very different fate, for today they owe much, if not all, of their vitality in popular custom to the church. There is some reason for supposing that the origin of the custom is to be sought in Germany. At least, Lippert[3] asserts that it is not mentioned prior to the ninth century and then in Germany. But it is not clear that this allusion has anything to do with Judas; indeed, so far as I can see he has in mind the prohibition by Pope Zacharias of the spring fires,[4] and in the absence of any very early instances in my collection which mention Judas I shall not venture any speculations on this point. The tenacity with which the custom is maintained along the shores of the Mediterranean, by Greeks and Portuguese particularly, can hardly be interpreted as supporting Lippert's notion, if it refers specifically to the burning of Judas as distinguished from the Easter fires in general, while, on the other hand, the absence of any evidence that the rite is known in France, except in Alsace, might be held to favor his contention.

On Easter Eve all lights in the church are extinguished and a new fire is kindled, sometimes with flint and steel, sometimes with a burning glass. With it the Easter or Paschal

---

[3] *Christenthum, Volksglaube und Volksbrauch*, Berlin, 1882, p. 482 citing Waldmann, *Eichfeldsche Gebräuche*, Programm, 1864, p. 6. See also Bronner (*Von deutscher Sitt' und Art*, Munich, 1908, pp. 130 ff.) who connects the Judaslied with this custom, holding that the song indicates the existence of a belief that Judas must be burning in hell-fire. On the *Judaslied* see my article, "O du armer Judas," *Journ. of Eng. and Germ. Philol.*, XIX (1920), 318-38. For the attitude of the church toward these spring fires see A. Franz, *Die kirchlichen Benediktionen im Mittelalter*, Freiburg i. B., 1909, I, 517 ff.

[4] See Jahn, *Die deutschen Opfergebräuche*, pp. 129 ff.

candle is lit, and then all the lights in the church are lit. Often a consecrated bonfire in an open space is set alight, from which the people bear away charred sticks for their own hearths. Some of the sticks are inserted in the roof to ward off lightning or are laid on the hearth-fire during thunderstorms. Gardens and crops are supposed to thrive when ashes from these fires are spread on the ground, applied to the plough, or mixed with the seed. Often an effigy, which is now and again called Judas, is burned in the consecrated bonfire, and in some places where no effigy is burned, the fire is nevertheless known as the "burning of Judas." Occasionally the effigy is called the "Ostermann," the Wandering Jew, Winter, or Death. Judas is, therefore, neither the original nor the only figure to be thus insulted. The original figure is doubtless to be seen in the personifications of Death and Winter.[5] Customs of this sort, in which the name of Judas appears, are reported from Greece, the Mediterranean shores, Germany, and the Catholic countries of the New World. The differences in the time of celebrating this ceremony are apparently of little consequence, and are here disregarded in favor of a geographical classification. The fires and processions are reported as occurring on the days immediately preceding Lent, on Laetare Sunday (the fourth Sunday in Lent), in connection with the solemnities of Good Friday and Easter, and (more rarely) on Low Sunday (the Sunday after Easter). But whatever the time there seems to be no question that the ceremony is a transformation of the pagan rites connected with the vernal equinox and the coming of Spring.

In and about the Mediterranean the custom of burning Judas seems still to flourish vigorously. So far as the evidence here collected goes, it would seem to be more popular among Roman Catholics than among Greek

[5] See in general Sartori, *Sitte und Brauch*, III, 130 ff.

Catholics. Sir J. G. Frazer who witnessed the ceremony in Greece in 1890 describes it as follows:

> At Athens, the new fire is kindled in the cathedral at midnight on Holy Saturday. A dense crowd with unlit candles in their hands fills the square in front of the cathedral; the king, the archbishop, and the highest dignitaries of the church, arrayed in their gorgeous robes, occupy a platform; and at the exact moment of the resurrection the bells ring out, and the whole square bursts as by magic into a blaze of light. Theoretically all the candles are lit from the sacred new fire in the cathedral, but practically it may be suspected that the matches which bear the name of Lucifer have some share in the sudden illumination. Effigies of Judas used to be burned at Athens on Easter Saturday, but the custom has been forbidden by the Government. However, firing goes on more or less continuously all over the city both on Easter Saturday and Easter Sunday, and the cartridges used on this occasion are not always blank. The shots are aimed at Judas, but they sometimes miss him and hit other people.[6]

He remarks further that he has a "photograph of a Theban Judas, dangling from a gallows and partially enveloped in smoke," which was taken during the Easter celebration of 1891. In Macedonia a similar custom existed until recently. And as late as 1902 a number of "Jews," meaning probably Judases, made of cast-off clothes and stuffed with straw, were burned at Therapia, the fashionable summer resort of Constantinople.[7] These rites, as the editor of *Notes and Queries* observes, seem to have aroused international difficulties about the middle of the past century:

> The question at present [1850] pending between this country [Great Britain] and Greece, so far as regards the claim of M. Pacifico, appears, from the papers laid before Parliament, to have had its origin in what Sir Edward Lyon states "to have been the custom in Athens for some years, to burn an effigy of Judas on Easter day." And from the account of the origin of the riots by the Council of the Criminal Court of Athens,

---

[6] *Op. cit.*, I, 130. Cf. his detailed description in *Folk-Lore*, I (1890), 275.

[7] G. F. Abbott, *Macedonian Folklore*, Cambridge, 1903, p. 37. He cites the *Daily Chronicle* of May 2, 1902, as authority for the scene at Therapia.

we learn, that "it is proved by the investigation, that on March 23, 1847, Easter Day, a report was spread in the parish of the Church des Incorporels, that the Jew, D. Pacifico, by paying the churchwarden of the church, succeeded in preventing the effigy of Judas from being burnt in that parish on Easter Day." From another document in the same collection it seems, that the Greek Government, out of respect to M. Charles de Rothschild, who was at Athens in April, 1847, forbid in all the Greek churches of the capital the burning of Judas.[8]

"On Easter Day," says Rouse, who writes on the folk-lore of the Sporades, "a straw image is made of Judas which is hung up, shot at with guns, and finally burnt."[9] In Corfu, which enjoys the melancholy honor of possessing the house of the traitor,[10] Judas is cursed on Easter Sunday while pieces of crockery are broken in the hope that the fragments will pierce his body.[11] Strangely enough the breaking of crockery to this laudable end is practised only here and in England, but there seems to be no connection between the customs. In Silesia the burning of Judas has degenerated into the throwing of broken pottery at a barrel and this development seems likewise to be an independent one. The Corfiote burning of Judas, a sort of Guy Fawkes celebration, takes place on Good Friday.[12] Another observer reports from Malta that the bells are rung on Good Friday, but he makes no mention of bonfires:

> The Maltese at Valletta . . . , on Good Friday Eve, have the custom of *jangling* the church bells with the utmost violence, in execration of the memory of Judas; and I have seen there a large wooden machine (of which they have many in use), constructed on a principle similar to that of an old-fashioned watchman's rattle, but of far greater

---

[8] *Notes and Queries*, 1st Ser., I, 357-8 (March 30, 1850).
[9] "Folk-lore from the Southern Sporades," *Folk-Lore*, X(1899), 178.
[10] See Paull F. Baum, "Roland 3220, 3220a," *Romanic Review*, VII (1916), 211-20.
[11] *Monthly Packet of Evening Readings for Younger Members of the English Church*, XXIII (1862), 133; see also Kirkwall, *Ionian Islands*, II, 47.
[12] Jaffery, *Notes and Queries*, 11th Ser., XI, 487 (June 26, 1915).

power in creating an uproar, intended to be symbolical of the rattling of *Judas's bones, that will not rest in his grave.*[13]

The straw puppet of Judas is still burned in Cyprus in much the same fashion as in Greece itself. There, too, the temptation to form the puppet in the image of some one was felt and in the early days of the English occupation the traitor bore an unmistakable resemblance to the English tourist. The ceremony is begun by the fire at the cathedral and later a puppet is burned in each of the Greek Catholic parishes. The efforts of the better educated Greeks to put an end to the custom have not met with much success.[14]

The sailors from the shores and islands of the Mediterranean carry their customs with them and have often flogged Judas in the harbor of London and elsewhere. The various graphic descriptions to which I have had access are given below. The first seems to have been taken from the *Boston Transcript*, which gives the *London News* as its source. The clipping may be dated shortly before or after 1900. It is as follows:

Yesterday the reenacting of the Good Friday custom of the flogging of an effigy of Judas Iscariot, the false apostle, was carried out with more than usual circumstance aboard a vessel moored in the "Pool."

For a long number of years the Mediterranean sailors attached to those trading vessels in the different London docks had been in the habit of celebrating their national custom of flogging, hanging and afterward burning the emblem of the "Betrayer," but owing to the disorder caused by the assemblage of roughs and loafers and consequent scenes of riot, and further the contravention of the fire regulations and its attendant danger, the authorities put a stop to the proceedings.

Until yesterday this order had obtained, but owing to the fact that the officers and men of a vessel moored in the "Pool" had signified

---

[13] Snow, *Notes and Queries*, 1st Series, I, 357(30 Mar., 1850). A similar custom is reported from the shores of the Rhine, on which see below and the article by Andree there mentioned.

[14] See Magda H. Ohnefalsch-Richter, *Griechische Sitten und Gebräuche auf Cypern*, Berlin, 1913, pp. 92-94. Note particularly the photographs reproduced on plates 25 and 26. Cf. also M. P. Nilsson, *Årets folkliga fester*, 1915, p. 1120.

their sympathy with the custom advantage was taken to celebrate the custom and without offending the law.

Accordingly, shortly after 11:30, a considerable number of Maltese and Portugese sailors boarded the boat, and taking a log of wood invested it with a sailor's "jumper" and a red knitted hat as nautical costume; they then proceeded to revile, kick and spit on the figure, and after a time a rope was placed around it, when it was hoisted to the masthead, and then immediately lowered on to the deck, where it was again subjected to every indignity possible, in which all heartily co-operated.

Rehoisted to the masthead, it was dropped thrice overboard, and being drawn on deck was summarily cut up and burned.

This Good Friday custom obtains among all Mediterranean seamen, and its revival in the "Pool" of London after a lapse of 20 years seemed to afford all concerned intense satisfaction.

A description of the custom as practised a generation earlier is very similar:

At daybreak [Good Friday] a block of wood, roughly carved to imitate the Betrayer, and clothed in an ordinary sailor's suit, with a red worsted cap on its head, was hoisted by a rope round its neck into the fore-rigging; the crews of the various vessels [Portuguese and South American] then went to chapel, and on their return, about 11 a. m., the figure was lowered from the rigging, and cast into the dock, and ducked three times. It was then hoisted on board, and after being kicked round the deck was lashed to the capstan. The crew, who had worked themselves into a state of frantic excitement, then with knotted ropes lashed the effigy till every vestige of clothing had been cut to tatters. During this process the ship's bell kept up an incessant clang, and the captains of the ships served out grog to the men. Those not engaged in the flogging kept up a rude sort of chant intermixed with denunciations of the Betrayer. The ceremony ended with the burning of the effigy amid the jeers of the crowd.[15]

---

[15] *London Times*, April 5, 1874 (quoted by T. F. T. Dyer, *British Popular Customs*, London, 1900, pp. 155-56 and W. S. Walsh, *Curiosities of Popular Customs*, Philadelphia, 1898, pp. 579-80). M. D. Conway (*Demonology and Devil-Lore*, London, 1879, I, 81) alludes to it. B. Taylor (*Storyology*, London, 1900, p. 107) mentions a performance of 1881. See also Ditchfield, *Old English Customs*, 1896, p. 76.

According to a Cork newspaper similar ceremonies were celebrated there about 1868. "The traitor was led through the streets in a solemn procession, twenty men marching in front singing an 'epithalamium,' as the reporter has chosen to call it. The effigy of Judas was laid on an open bier arranged in the blue shirt and long boots of a stevedore. On returning to the ship the effigy was hung to the yardarm and fired into with pistols."[16] The custom, we are told, is known also in Portugal and Madeira. At Lisbon a penitential silence reigns on Good Friday. Grotesquely attired figures appear before each house on Saturday. Here and there the figure of the traitor is accompanied by that of a woman. The bell of the cathedral gives the signal for the lighting of these effigies of straw, which burn readily until they are blown apart by the powder contained within. Such ceremonies were officially forbidden in Madeira in 1889, for the effigies had come to resemble a little too closely the physical appearance of certain local officials.

The practice is still (1920) a familiar one in the Cape Verde islands. "Easter morning about four o'clock a fig-tree[17] is planted on one side of the church. On it is hung a straw-stuffed figure of a man called Juda. A cigar is put in his mouth and a bomb on his chest. About noon, when the day's procession from the church is at hand, the bomb is exploded by the fuse held in the mouth of the figure. All the men drag the tree and the figure, or what is left of it, by a rope around the shore. Here they beat the figure and then drown it (Fogo). In Cab' Verde the figure of Juda is paraded on a donkey and beaten. It is paraded, beaten, and burned in Brava."[18]

[16] Walsh, *loc. cit.* (quoting the *Cork Examiner*).
[17] Alluding, no doubt, to the tradition which associates the suicide of the traitor with the fig-tree; see my paper, "The Gallows of Judas Iscariot," *Washington University Studies*, IX (1922), Humanistic Series, 135-56.
[18] Parsons, "Folk-Lore of the Cape Verde Islanders," *Journ. Am. Folk-Lore*, XXXIV (1921), 105-6.

A somewhat different custom, called appropriately enough "Thrashing Judas Iscariot," prevails in the church of Santa Croce, Florence on Good Friday. All the boys of the city buy on that morning long willow rods tied with colored ribbons, and take them with them to church. At a certain point in the service, they loudly beat the benches with them.[19] Parallels to this custom will be found in abundance north of the Alps, but I have not noted anything similar to this, where there is no burning of an effigy, in the Mediterranean countries.

It is no doubt merely accident that I have failed to turn up any instances of the burning of Judas in Spain. There is every reason to believe that it is as familiar there as in Portugal. Professor Joseph E. Gillet, to whom I am indebted for the following material, tells me that in Spain the ceremony is performed on Holy Thursday. Its great popularity in Mexico and in South America generally is evidence of a well-established Spanish custom. In certain parts of Spain the straw effigy is called "el despensero" (the steward), alluding to the tradition that Judas was the steward of the twelve.[20]

We may now leave the south of Europe and cross the Alps. In central Europe the custom of burning Judas seems to be known chiefly in German-speaking lands. It is reported from Luxemburg, where it is practised by peasants who speak a German dialect; from all parts of Germany itself and particularly from those regions in which there is still a substantial Catholic representation; from Alsace; from Switzerland, where it seems to be best known in the northern, German-speaking portion; and from

---

[19] E. L. Urlin, *Festivals, Holy Days, and Saints' Days*, London, 1915, p. 64.

[20] See Luís Vélez de Guevara, *Diablo cojuelo* (ed. Rodríguez Marín), II, 61. Perhaps connected with this tradition is the representation of Judas as wearing boots, as Quevedo (*Sueños*, ed. Cejador, I, 144) suggests, because Judas, being a "despensero," was always on the go.

Bohemia, where it has been adopted from the Germans by the Czechs. Instances from France appear to be lacking, although the custom must once have been familiar there, for the French have carried it to one of their colonies in the New World.

In Luxemburg (Vianden) a boy bearing a hawthorn twig adorned with ribbons leads a crowd of boys swinging rattles. From time to time they stop and cry: "Jaudes, Jaudes, Spackeldâr, iwermuor as Oschterdâch! (Judas, Judas, Hawthorn thorn, day after tomorrow is Easter.)" Elsewhere (Diekirch) the children cry on the same occasion:

> Zu hâf, zu hâf,
> De Jekdes as entlâf!
> (Come here, come here,
> Judas has escaped.)[21]

The reviling of Judas, taking form, usually during Holy Week, either in a bonfire or in an outburst of noise and disorder, is a very well attested bit of popular custom in Germany. Here it is found, earlier than anywhere else and here it is still widely distributed in a variety of local forms. I give first the allusions to the rite prior to the nineteenth century and then group the more recent instances geographically. Martin Luther is, so far as I am aware, the first one to make mention of the Rumpelmette, a riotous celebration within the walls of the church. He says: "Zcum ersten bedenken ettlich das leyden Christi alsso, dass sie über die Juden tzornig werden, singen und schelten über den armen Judas."[22] The phrase "den armen Judas" is certainly a reminiscence of the Judas song, "O du armer Judas, was hast du getan?", which as we shall see is still

---

[21] E. de la Fontaine, *Luxemburger Sitten und Bräuche*, Luxemburg, 1883, p. 38.

[22] "Sermon von der Betrachtung des heiligen Leidens Christi (1519)," *Werke* (Weimar Ausg.), II, 137.

sung in this connection in Bohemia.[23] Two generations later the Low German reformer and preacher, Niklaus Gryse, shows his knowledge of this custom and of its characteristic name, "Judasjagen." He described it as follows:

> An den beyden nafolgenden dagen [nach Palmsonntag], holdt men de Rumpelmetten, vnd lüdet mit holteren Klocken, den Sekenklappen gelyck, welckere Instrument Raspelen genömet werden. Ock jagen se den Judam mit stöken vnd steinen stormende herumme, alse dulle vnd vulle verblendede lüde.[24]

In the next century the Alsatian Johann Fischart, who translated and enlarged Gargantua, alludes to the "Judasjagen," another name for the "Rumpelmette," in a truly Rabelaisian passage:

> Wenn man ausz deiner nasen ein leiter macht, das man ein vasz voll treck darauf im keller ziehe, und dein hals zum schlauch, zum ablasz, da würden sich die hufer recht regen, als wann die wirt mit der ketten im fasz rumpeln und die drusen judasjagen.[25]

And in his *Binenkorb* he mentions the custom again:

> Inn der Marterwochen aigt man trei Nächt nacheinander den Judas, finster inn der Rumpelmetten mit Hämmern, steynen, schlegeln, klüpffeln, kolben, stecken, poltern, stossen und klopffen, so unsinnig als stürmten die teuffel das Fegfeuer.[26]

The phrase "Judas verbrennen," which is quoted by Birlinger from a curious eighteenth century book on the rites of the Catholic church, is accompanied by an explana-

---

[23] See my discussion "'O du armer Judas,'" *Journ. Eng. and Germ. Philol.*, XIX (1920), 318-38.

[24] *Spegel des Pawestdoms*, 1593, "De I. Bede." See the references cited by U. Jahn, *Opfergebräuche*, p. 130, n. 2.

[25] P. 135ª. Quoted by Haltaus, *Glossarium germ. medii aevi*, Leipzig, 1758, *s.v.* Judasjagen. I have not located the passage in Alsleben's edition (Neudrucke deutscher Literaturwerke, Nos. 65-76, Halle, 1891). See also the references given by Wendeler (*Korrespondenzbl. f. nd. Sprachf.*, V [1880], 47-8, n. 6).

[26] Ed. Christlingen, 1581, ii, c. xvi, p. 150 a.

tion which seems to be incorrect. The passage in question is as follows:

> Neubekehrter: Wolan denn, was heisst das: Judas verbrennen?
> Doctor: das ist ein alt Sprichwort, welches weiter nichts bedeutet, als dass Judas, so auss Meineid Christum verkauft und verraten, in der Höll nun brenne und brate, gleichwie der Priester das alte hl. Oehl durch das feuer verzehren lässt.[27]

The reviling or burning of Judas at Easter is well known along the course of the Rhine, although the custom appears now to be falling into disuse. It has given in Cologne a name to spring housecleaning, locally called "den Judas ausfegen."[28] In that city the children used to go about during Holy Week to gather wood with which to burn the "Judas," a straw effigy of the traitor borne about on a long staff. They swung rattles and sang a song in which, however, Judas was not mentioned. When enough wood had been collected, they went to an open place, built a bonfire, and in it burnt the effigy. The song, in a version taken down about 1840, is as follows:

> Rohden, Rohden, Eichhôn,
> gitt mer get en et Zeuchhôn!
> Rohden dit, Rohden dat,
> gitt mer en dä Knappsack.
> Mûs, Mûs, kom erûs,
> breng mer ä gross Stöck Holz erûs.
> O gitt mer bald get![29]

---

[27] *Alemannia*, II (1875), 144 (from Rippel, *Alterthumb, Ursprung und Bedeutung aller Ceremonien, Gebräuchen und Gewohnheiten der Heiligen catholischen Kirchen*, Strassburg, 1723). For a fuller title and a characterization of the volume see Birlinger, *ibid.*, I(1873), 194.

[28] Wrede, *Rheinische Volkskunde*, 1919, p. 185.

[29] Erk and Böhme, *Deutscher Liederhort*, II(Leipzig, 1894), 139, No. 1230, "Das Judasliedchen aus Köln." They give the melody. On this song see further: Simrock, *Rheinland*, 2nd ed., p. 346 (cited by Hildebrand, *Materialien*, p. 63, n. 1); J. W. Wolf, *Beiträge*, I(1852), 74 (with minor variations in the spelling); Firmenich, *Germaniens Völkerstimmen*, I, 458; Weyden, *Cöln vor 50 Jahren*, p. 127; Erk, *Die deutschen Volkslieder mit ihren Singweisen*, II, 6, 40; F. M. Böhme, *Deutsches Kinder-*

Should any one refuse, they sing: "Et sitz en Schwalfter op dem Dach, de driess der Frau en Aug ûs, en Aug ûs, en Aug ûs." The police, says Wolf (1852), have since forbidden the rite. Not far away, in the Eifel mountains, the "Jaudesjagen" is described simply as an uproar in the church, the "Rumpelmette." On Easter morning, after the priest has walked thrice about the church and has reentered it, the boys of the parish are accustomed to make an uproar at a suitable place in the church. The commentator sees in this act an imitation of the earthquake at the Crucifixion—but the suggestion need hardly be taken seriously.[30] In certain Westphalian villages the boys gather in the schoolroom where they await the stroke of midnight on Saturday to begin stamping on the floor, beating on the benches, swinging wooden rattles, and shouting.[31] This they call "Judasjagen," a word which, as we have seen, Fischart knew three centuries before.

About the middle of the last century a correspondent of *Notes and Queries* says: "On Good Friday Eve the children at Boppart, on the Rhine, in Germany have the custom of

lied und Kinderspiel, 1897, p. 343 (remarks that the title in Erk and Böhme is without authority); J. Müller, "Schäälen Zacheies [schielender Zachäus]," Zs. des Ver. f. rhein. u. westf. Volkskunde, III (1906), 85-86; Beiheft to Archiv für Religionswissenschaft, VIII, 95; Zs. des Vereins f. Volkskunde. V (1895), 112 (with severe criticism of the foolish explanations of the text).

The allusion to the squirrel (*Eichhôn*) seems to refer to a lost custom or rite. Sartori collects some scattering allusions in *Sitte und Brauch*, III, 140, n. 6. See further on this point: Grimm, *Deutsche Mythologie*, p. 582; *Folk-Lore*, XIV (1903), 85; E. L. Urlin, *Festivals*, p. 64; T. F. T. Dyer, *British Popular Customs*, pp. 404, 430; Jahn, *Die deutschen Opfergebräuche*, pp. 123, 135, 267. Chasing the red squirrel is called "hunting Judas" in England; see Whistler, "Local Traditions of the Quantocks," *Folk-Lore*, XIX (1908), 41. The explanation that the red squirrels are in some way connected with Judas, who has red hair, need hardly be taken seriously. And I am equally uncertain about the opinion which relates them to the red haired god Thor.

[30] Schmitz, *Sitten, Sagen und Lieder . . . des Eifler Volkes*, II, 27 (cited by Hildebrand, *Materialien*, p. 63). Sartori (III, 139, n. 3) gives the reference as to vol. I.

[31] P. Sartori, *Westfälische Volkskunde*, 1922, p. 153.

making a most horrid noise with *rattles*. They call it *breaking the bones of Judas*."[32] A little further south, at Bretzenheim near Mainz, the boys of the village were accustomed as late as the decade 1860-70 to mark the beginning of the Roman Catholic service by going about the streets when the bells had ceased ringing. They carried rattles and other noise-makers. This was continued throughout Holy Week. On Saturday, when the Easter fire burned before the church, they cried to the sound of the rattles: "Jaurus, Jaurus werd verbrennt." The coals which were carried home from the fire were called "Jauruskohle." The writer adds that he is unaware of any superstitious use of the coals.[33] The burning of Judas was practised in the Palatinate in the first half of the century and could even be seen in a few villages of that district as late as 1907.[34] But there, too, the ceremony is doomed to an early death.

The existence of the custom of burning Judas is particularly well attested in Alsace. Fischart's familiarity with it has already been remarked and since his day there have been many to report the practice. About 1850, we are told,[35] it was usual to collect old crosses from the cemeteries and burn them with a "Judas." At Nellingen a fire was lit in the churchyard or beside the church before mass on the Saturday preceding Easter. The priest blessed the fire and from it the candles in the church were lit. Popularly the fire was known as the "Judasfeuer" and it was customary to say, "The faithless apostle is being burned."[36] In Liebsdorf

[32] Janus Dousa, 1st Ser., ii, 511 (28 Dec., 1850).
[33] *Hessische Blätter f. Volkskunde*, III (1904), 162-63.
[34] Becker, *Hessische Blätter*, VII (1907), 150, 169 citing J. Grentz, *Ensheim vor 60 Jahren*, Forbach, 1894, p. 19; F. Panzer, *Bayerische Sagen und Bräuche*, II, 531, 533. Panzer's remarks concern the Easter fires in general; Grentz I have not seen.
[35] Stöber, *Alsatia*, 1852, p. 131.
[36] *Jahrbuch f. Geschichte, Sprache u. Litt. Elsass-Lothringens*, II (1886), 185.

(formerly Kreis Altkirch) fragments of consecrated objects and fallen crucifixes from the graves are burned on Saturday before the church. Then it is said: "Der ewige Jud wird verbrannt," implying probably Judas and not Ahasuerus.[37] At Roppenzweiler, also in what was Kreis Altkirch, a fire is made, near the church, of old crosses and wood from the church tower. This, however, takes place on Good Friday about six in the morning. Every one takes a coal or a nail from the fire to lay in the stable to keep the Devil from the cattle. The rite is termed "den roten Juden verbrennen."[38] Because of the association of Judas with the color red there can be no doubt that the traitor is here intended.[39] The ritual at Steinsulz in the same region prescribes the lighting of the fire (on Saturday) by striking flints; in it old crosses are burned. The villagers say: "Der rote Jud wird verbrennt."[40] At Berghozzell (Kreis Gebweiler) the burning of fallen crosses and fragments of coffins occurs on Saturday. Everyone brings posts from the vineyards and lays them in the flames. These charred posts are later kept in the stables and stalls to protect the cattle The custom is called "den Jud verbrennen."[41] There is every reason to believe that the "Jew" and the "red Jew" are no other than Judas, for the confusion of *Jud* and *Judas* is a ready one in German. The same phrase is used when Judas is surely meant. Thus, it is used as "Der Judas wird verbrannt" of the fire on Saturday before Easter in Biederthal, which is in the previously mentioned Kreis Altkirch.[42] At Mittebronn (Kreis Saarburg) "Judas" is burned in the churchyard while the boys of the village

---

[37] *Ibid.*, VI (1890), 166.
[38] *Ibid.*, VIII (1892), 162.
[39] See Baum, *Journ. Eng. and Germ. Ph.*, XXI (1922), 520-29.
[40] *Jahresb. f. Gesch., Spr., u. Lit. Elsass-Lothringens*, X (1894), 226.
[41] *Ibid.*
[42] *Jahrbuch*, III (1887), 125.

hammer with the utmost violence "to injure Judas as much as possible."[43] This custom of hammering we have already met on the Rhine and we shall find it peculiarly favored by the folk in Bavaria.

We may now cross the Rhine and turn our attention eastward, noting by the way the existence of a few allusions to related customs in Switzerland. There, in Einsiedeln, the Easter fire, which is known as "Judasverbrennen," is kindled on the Saturday before Easter. Flint and tinder must be used, and the fire is consecrated by the priest. It is believed that the coal possesses magic power.[44] To the north, in Baden, the custom is still known, although it is fast dying out. The straw man burned at Oberlanda bears the name "Judas,"[45] and the Easter fire at Mergentheim in Swabia is called the "Judasverbrennen."[46] At Ettlingenweier logs are dragged to the fire in which the "Judas" is burned. Later the partially charred fragments are carried home to protect the house against lightning and fire. The priest consecrates the fire at Unzhurst (Bühl), and here the fragments of the consecrated palms are burned.[47]

In the village of Schluchtern, we are told, the priest consecrates on Saturday outside of the church a fire to which all or almost all of the community contributes billets. After they have been charred the fire is extinguished and the fragments of the wood are carried home where they are laid away in the rafters for a year.[48]

Further north, in the central German district of Eichsfeld, Easter ceremonies are varied in character. In some villages

---

[43] *Jahrbuch*, III (1887), 125.

[44] E. Hoffmann-Krayer, *Schweizerisches Archiv f. Volksk.*, XI (1907), 246; see *ibid.*, VIII, 313. For the Rumpelmette in Switzerland see below, p. 179, n. 60.

[45] E. H. Meyer, *Badisches Volksleben*, Strassburg, 1900, p. 98.

[46] Birlinger, *Volkstümliches aus Schwaben*, II, 62.

[47] Meyer, *ibid.*

[48] M. Ruckert, "Aus Schluchtern," *Mein Heimatland; Badische Blätter f. Volkskunde*, VII (1920), 54.

a straw puppet called Judas was burned. Curiously enough the ashes of this fire are held to be injurious and are thrown into a brook. The collections for the Easter fire are made by boys who sing on their rounds. One of the songs which is employed on this occasion has been preserved and is sufficiently characteristic to justify reprinting from the inaccessible periodical in which it first appeared:

> Es sangen drei Engel einen süssen Gesang,
> Sie sangen, dass es zum Himmel erklang!
> Da unser Herr Christus zu Tische sass
> Und mit den zwölf Jüngern das Abendmahl ass,
> Stand auch der Verräter Judas dabei:
> Er sollte auf ewig verloren sein.
> Da ging unser Herre den Ölberg hinauf
> Und weckte die lieben Jüngerlein auf:
> „Wachet auf, wachet auf, gehet alle mit mir,
> Meine Zeit und Stunde ist kommen allhier."
>
> Es stand ein Sünder wohl an der Tür,
> Wie traurig, wie traurig stand er dafür.
> „Ach Sünder, ach Sünder, was trauerst du?
> Wenn mein Auge dich sieht, was weinest du?"
> „Soll ich nicht weinen, mein Herr und Gott?
> Ich habe gebrochen die zehen Gebot."
> „Hast du sie gebrochen, die zehen Gebot,
> „So fall auf deine Knie und bete zu Gott,
> Und bete und bete nur alle Zeit,
> So wird dir Gott schenken die Seligkeit!
> Im Himmel, im Himmel sind der Freuden gar viel,
> Da singen die Engel und haben ihr Spiel."[49]

Throughout the Allgäu, a district including the highlands of southern Württemberg and Bavaria, the spring fires are lit on a day called variously "Funkentag," "Funkensonntag," "Scheibentag," and "der weisse Sonntag" (not

---

[49] W. Kolde, "Osterbrauch und Osterspiele auf dem Eichsfelde," *Niedersachsen*, IX (1903-4), 213.

to be confused with "der weisse Sonntag" after Easter), which is always the first Sunday in Lent. The wood for the fire is gathered from bushes and underbrush and not, as in Alsace, from the churchyard. Wheels or discs wrapped with tow and dipped in pitch are rolled through the fire and down the hill. Youths and maidens dance about the fire and jump through it. In the center is often erected a post or cross enveloped in straw, which is called "die Hex" (the witch) and when this catches fire the climax of the rite is attained. The ceremony is thought to assure prosperity for the following season and to make certain that the couples which jump through the fire together will remain mutually attached during the coming year. Although the rite is rather widely known in the Allgäu it is called "Judasbrennen" in only a few villages (Bernbeuren, Burggen, Altenstedt).[50] At Gmünd, in Württemberg, there is a strange procession which is of interest in this connection: On Holy Thursday the twelve poorest men in the village, who are on this occasion called apostles, dress themselves in gray, and have the privilege of begging at every house. The one representing Judas marches ahead with a purse.[51] This seems to be rather a relic of an old Easter play than a fragment of the spring festival. It may be remarked that there is a similar procession in the Frisian territory of Saterland (northwestern Germany). The man who receives the gifts of sausage on a long pole is called "Wurstelberend"; the one who bears a bee-hive for the eggs, "Eierulk"; and the treasurer, the

---

[50] K. Reiser, *Sagen, Gebräuche und Sprichwörter des Allgäus*, Kempten, II, 99, cf. pp. 93 ff. See also J. Gross, "Charsamstags-Feuer," *Deutsche Gaue*, XIV (1913), 200. According to Gross the ceremony has been forbidden in the districts of Dachau, Friedberg, and Bruck.

[51] Birlinger, *Volkstümliches aus Schwaben*, II, 77 (cited by Sartori, III, 140); this is surely the passage from which Auricoste de Lazarque, "Le Grundonnerstag ou le jeudi vert en Alsace-Lorraine et en Allemagne," *Rev. des trad. pop.*, VIII (1893), 541 draws his information. For analogous ceremonies in which Judas does not play so important a rôle see Sartori, III, 140, n. 10.

receiver of the moneys, "Judas."⁵² In both of these instances the practice of asking a dole, which may or may not be a part of the spring-festival, has become independent, and has acquired a certain individuality. We need only remark the presence of Judas.

In Bavaria the Judas fire, to which the folk was summoned by the cry "Brennen wir den Judas!"⁵³ had the ostensible purpose of averting hail-storms. In this instance the original intent of the rite, the benefiting of the husbandman, is still apparent. Early in the last century the authorities forbade its celebration, probably not because they realized its hidden paganism but because, as elsewhere, of the opportunities for misconduct it gave the young people. The youths of the village of Althenneberg, as Wolf describes the custom,⁵⁴ gathered wood on Saturday before Easter. A cross was made from a tall pole, enveloped in straw, planted in the ground, and encircled with the wood of the pyre. In the evening after the service in the church the youths lit their lanterns from the consecrated fire of the church and ran at full speed to the pile of wood. The first to arrive was allowed to light the bonfire. No woman was permitted to approach it. Two youths were appointed to watch it throughout the night and to protect it from theft. At sunrise the ashes were gathered and thrown into the Rötenbach. The man who had reached the pile first was honored on Easter day with a donation of colored eggs at the

---

⁵² W. Lüpkes, *Ostfriesische Volkskunde*, 1907, p. 148; Strackerjan, *Aberglaube u. Sagen aus dem Herzogtum Oldenburg*, 2nd ed. by Willoh, Oldenburg, 1909, II, 60-61, No. 304.

⁵³ Karl Blind's suggestion that this is a corruption of "Brennen wir den Jötun!" calls for no comment; see "Wodan, der wilde Jäger und der wandernde Ahasver," *Deutsche Revue*, IV, iv (Aug., 1880), 195. In the same spirit is Wolf's equating of the Judasbrennen with the burning of Thor, because both are reputed to have red hair; see *Beiträge*, I, 72 and K. A. Oberle, *Ueberreste germanischen Heidentums*, Baden-Baden, 1883, pp. 108, 117.

⁵⁴ *Beiträge zur deutschen Mythologie*, I (1852), 72-73, quoting Panzer, *Bayerische Sagen und Bräuche*, I, 212-13, No. 236.

church door. At Freising and in other localities the phrase used of these fires is "den Ostermann brennen," in which it is not certain that the "Easter man" is Judas. According to a prohibition of the practice issued by Duke Maximilian in 1611 it was the Devil whose image was thrown down and torn to bits by the common people in the belief that the rags and fragments would protect their fields from hail.[55] The name "Judasbrennen" is often preserved, although, as in the Lechrain and Tirol, the puppet has been done away with. In the Lechrain[56] the church is visited on the morning of the Saturday before Easter as on an ordinary workday, with the exception that each household sends a stick of wood to the fire which is lit before the church. The fire must have been kindled by flint and tinder. The custom was called as late as 1855 "den Judas verbrennen," although there is neither symbol nor mention of him during the ceremony. We are told, moreover, that there is usually no noise or singing by the children on the way to the bonfire, and in this particular the ceremony differs markedly from most of those described. The fire is extinguished and the charred billet is carried home as a valuable object. Later in the year when a storm rises the billet is laid on the fire so that the smoke it gives off may serve as a protection from the lightning. The consecrated wood has yet other virtues: it can injure a man who is defended by a charm against hurt from ordinary weapons, or if a stove is bewitched, a few live coals from the billet will kindle a fire that will satisfy the

[55] Cf. Mannhardt, *Antike Wald- und Feldkulte*, I, 305, n. 2; Panzer, *Bayerische Sagen*, II, 281, No. 28; U. Jahn, *Opfergebräuche*, p. 153. In northern Baden it is the Wandering Jew who is burnt; cf. Heilig, *Zs. d. Ver. f. Volkskunde*, XX (1910), 399. In Brandenburg the figure is called "Alt Adam"; cf. E. Friedel, "Ostergebräuche im alten Berlin," *Brandenburgia*, XVI, 166-68. Cf. W. Kolde, "Osterbrauch und Osterspiele auf dem Eichsfelde," *Niedersachsen*, IX (1903-4), 213. A longer list can be readily compiled from the handbooks on popular customs.

[56] Leoprechting, *Aus dem Lechrain*, Munich, 1855, p. 172. See also L. von Hörmann, *Tiroler Volksleben*, Stuttgart, 1909, p. 59.

most critical. Ignaz von Zingerle reports the burning of Judas on the Saturday before Easter as being practised in Tirol about 1870.[57] The charred wood is buried under the threshold of the stable-door, for it is believed that this affords protection against witches and prevents cows from giving bloody milk.

Above the village of Eisingersdorf (Aichach, Oberbayern) there was erected as late as 1911 a large black, wooden cross, locally called "der Jaudas," i. e. "der Judas." It was soaked with tar and oil before its ignition on the Saturday preceding Easter. Unfortunately the description does not mention what the intent of the ceremony may have been. From this elevation, the "Nagelberg," other similar fires could be seen.[58]

In Bavaria the "Rumpelmette" enjoys an unusual popularity. Panzer defines it as follows: "The 'Pumpermetten,' a choral song, which now occurs in evenings of Thursday, Friday, and Saturday of Holy Week, were formerly celebrated in the horae matutinae. Formerly the church goers beat on the benches and walls with sticks, hammers, staves, and stones and uproar was held to be occasioned by the thought of Judas."[59] In Tirol the "Dammermette" is celebrated during the last days of Holy Week. Clubs are kept hidden behind the altar until the last candle is extinguished. Then any one is privileged to take one or two and pound and hammer ("dammern") to his heart's content. The noise is supposed to express the horror of the congregation at the crime of Judas.[60] In Silesian villages,

[57] *Sitten, Meinungen und Bräuche des Tiroler Volkes*, Innsbruck, 1871, p. 149, No. 1286.
[58] H. Müller, *Deutsche Gaue*, XV (1914), 125. The other villages in the neighborhood where the custom was still practised were, he says, Pichl and Edenhausen.
[59] *Bayerische Sagen und Bräuche*, II, 554-55.
[60] L. von Hörmann, *Tiroler Volksleben*, Stuttgart, p. 53; cf. Andree, *Zs. d. Ver. f. Volksk.*, XX (1910), 259, who compares it to the Hebrew custom of killing Haman

we are told, the sexton, who wore a red vest to represent Judas, used to appear on the extinguishing of the last candle. The boys drove him out of the church with shouts. Around Leobschütz boys run about in the fields while it is growing dark on Ash Wednesday. They carry with them brooms which have been dipped in tar. With the lighted brooms they set fire to hay-ricks and play other pranks. This they call "a Judassuchen" or "Judassehen."[61] Elsewhere in the same province it is known inappropriately enough as "Christussuchen." Philo von Walde, a Silesian dialect poet of considerable local fame, calls the practise "Judensehen," but this is obviously a corruption.[62] In both Austrian Silesia (at Wagstadt) and in German Silesia (at Strehlen) an attack upon the traitor is enacted. The sole difference seems to be that it takes place in Austria on the Wednesday before Easter and in Germany three days later, on Saturday. A disguised youth with blackened face, who has taken his stand on the steps of the tomb of the Augustinian monastery, is dragged hither and thither through the cemetery until the fathers put an end to the sport. Elsewhere in this region we find instead of the figure of the traitor a living cat or goat which is thrown down from the churchtower.[63] Here the substitution of the Biblical figure for the

with hammers at Purim; see also Sartori, *Sitte und Brauch*, III, 139 ff.; Wahner, "Zum Klappern gehen in der Karwoche," *Mitt. d. schles. Ges. f. Volksk.*, VI, no. 11, (1904), 73–77, and Grimm, *Deutsches Wörterbuch*, VIII, 1488, *s.v.* Rumpelmette; VII, 1993, *s.v.* Polterpassion; VII, 2231, *s.vv.* Pumpermette, Pumpermittwoch, Pumpernickel, 3; *Korrespondenzbl. f. niederdeutsche Sprachforschung*, II, 26 ff., III, 67, V, 46; Lippert, *Christenthum*, pp. 614-15. An interesting early description is quoted from the *Schweizerische Kirchenordnung* of 1588 in the *Schweizerisches Idiotikon*, I, 582, *s.v.* Ostere, 1, d.

[61] Dittrich, "Schlesische Opfergebräuche," *Mitteilungen d. schlesischen Gesellschaft f. Volkskunde*, I, Nr. 2 (1895-96), 10. Cf. Drechsler, *Sitte, Brauch und Volksglauben in Schlesien*, I, 78.

[62] U. Jahn, *Opfergebräuche*, p. 126 citing Philo von Walde, *Schlesien in Sage und Brauch*, p. 124.

[63] Görlich, *Geschichte der Stadt Strehlen*, p. 265 as quoted in P. Drechsler, *Brauch und Volksglaude in Schlesien*, I, 94.

earlier, less individualised one is quite obvious. It is strange to note that in Silesia alone, so far as I know, such ceremonies as these are celebrated on Easter Sunday itself. Here in many communities the services in memory of the resurrection take place before sun-rise on Easter morning and they are often followed by the "burning of Judas."[64] A strange corruption of the custom is found in various towns and villages of Silesia. Here the original purpose of the rite, the ensuring of a favorable season in the coming year, is completely obscured. In Glogau, for example, boys carry a barrel to a certain spot in the cemetery where they bombard it with stones and broken pottery until it caves in.

Having thus reached Silesia, we may cross the border and examine the customs in Bohemia which have reference to Judas. Formerly all liberal books were burned on Holy Thursday in the same fire with the "Judaspuppe."[65] Elsewhere in that country the boys of the village are allowed, beginning with Holy Thursday, to announce the Angelus. Usually when they have finished they kneel before the cross in the village square and recite the rosary. Often they accompany the beating of their rattle with couplets, of which one is as follows, "The infidel Jews are as black as dogs. They have dug a pit to take Christ, to crucify Him, and put Him in the Holy Sepulchre on Good Friday, to exhume him on Saturday. Infidel Judas, why did you deliver your Master to the Jews? As punishment, you now burn in Hell; there you shall remain with the Devil."[66] A little further East among the Slovaks, the burning of

---

[64] P. Drechsler, *op. cit.*, I, 93-94.

[65] Meissner, *Roccocobilder*, Gumbinnen, 1871, p. 61 (cited by Creizenach, *Beiträge zur Gesch. d. deutschen Sprache u. Litt.*, II, 184, n. 5).

[66] Rybak, "Traditions et coutumes chez les Tchécho-slaves: Du nouvel an à Pâques," *Rev. des trad. pop.*, XVIII (1903), 327. The passage beginning with "Infidel Judas" is the oft-mentioned Judas song.

Judas must be a familiar rite, for the peasants are said to throw a "Judaskohle," a bit of charcoal from the Easter fire, into the mouth of the Wassermandl to exorcise him when he appears in the shape of a dog.[67] In the county of Jičin the leader of the Judas chase is a red haired boy.[68]

Quite different from anything that has gone before is a West Bohemian custom in the region of Sanderauer. There the farmer goes about his field carrying consecrated palm twigs, crosses cut from the *Gudas* (i. e., Judas), and a jug of holy water. At each corner of the field he sets up a twig and a cross. During the perambulation he repeats the Gospel of John.[69] In this instance the Christianisation of the ancient heathen ritual of fertility has been carried to the farthest point. In a work on the peasant of the Bohemian forest we are told more about the preparation of the crosses used in this ceremony. On the Saturday before Easter a pyre is erected in front of the church and into it are cast the remnants of the sacramental oils and cotton. Women and children thrust the ends of billets into the fire for consecration. On Easter morning the charred billet is split, some of it is used for making a fire and the rest is made into crosses. On Monday the crosses are planted in the grain to ensure its growth and quality.[70]

English tradition, too, preserves reminiscences of fires in which effigies of Judas were burnt. In Hereford, "the fires are designed to represent the Savior and his apostles, and it was customary for one of them, held as representing Judas Iscariot, to allow it to burn a while, and then to put it

---

[67] Schukowitz, "Mythen und Sagen des Marchfeldes," *Zs. f. österr. Volksk.*, II (1896), 70.

[68] Reinsberg-Düringsfeld, *Böhmen*, 123 (cited by Sartori, III, 140); also cited in Floegel, *Geschichte des grotesk-komischen*⁵ (ed. Ebeling), p. 219.

[69] E. F. Knuchel, *Die Umwandlung in Kult, Magie und Rechtsbrauch*, 1919, p. 76 citing *Zs. f. österreichische Volksk.*, III, 112.

[70] J. Schramek, *Der Böhmerwaldbauer*, Prag, 1915, pp. 147-48 (Krummauer Gegend).

out and kick about the materials."[71] From the context it seems that this fire was lit on January 5th, a surprisingly early date which suggests connecting it with the midwinter rather than the spring fires. The identification of the fire and the traitor is a curious twist to the tradition which I cannot parallel in other accounts. In Cornwall the "burning of Judas" was formerly practised, although it was only a memory two generations ago. "The beginning of Lent," says Mrs. Whitcombe,[72] "was once marked by a custom now obsolete. A figure made of straw and old clothes was drawn through the streets, with much shouting and many followers. After this procession, it was either shot at, or thrown down a chimney. This image was called 'Jack o' Lent' and was evidently intended to represent Judas Iscariot." An analogous tradition avers that "it is lucky to break a piece of pottery on Good Friday because the points of the pieces are supposed to pierce the body of Judas Iscariot."[73]

Curiously enough this ceremony of burning Judas, which is the transformation of a pagan rite, has been borne to the New World by the Catholic church. It is met with in Mexico, in South America, and on some islands of the

---

[71] Chambers, *Book of Days*, I, 56 (Jan. 5th) whence the passage is taken in E. M. Leather, *Folklore of Herefordshire*, Hereford, 1912, pp. 91 ff. Miss Leather and Chambers mention other fires, which, however, do not seem to be associated with Judas in any way.

[72] *Bygone Days in Devonshire and Cornwall, with Notes of Existing Superstitions and Customs*, London, 1874, p. 188. On Jack o'Lent see also T. F. T. Dyer, *British Popular Customs*, pp. 92-93 citing *Notes and Queries*, 1st Ser., xii, 297 and Ben Jonson's *Tale of a Tub*.

[73] S. Hewett, *Nummits and Crummits*, London, 1900, p. 50; cf. E. M. Wright, *Rustic Speech and Folklore*, London, 1913, p. 22 (Miss Wright gives no reference for the belief; her authority is perhaps the passage quoted from Hewett). See also T. F. T. Dyer, *British Popular Customs*, pp. 76-77, " 'Lent Crocking' on Shrove Tuesday," in which, however, Judas is not mentioned. Crockery is also broken in northern Germany, cf. A. F. Rusch, "Ein Opferbrauch in Amte Ritzebüttel," *Niedersachsen*, IV (1898-9), 207.

West Indies. In Mexico City[74] the new fire is struck from a flint early in the morning of Easter Saturday, and a candle lighted from it is carried through the city church by a deacon shouting "Lumen Christi." The city has meanwhile prepared for the celebration. Effigies of Judas, dolls of Spanish and Aztec types, dangle from every house or are suspended from ropes which extend across the streets. Larger figures are stuffed with gunpowder and squibs or with meat, bread, soap, and clothing for which the crowd scuffle. The signal is given by the ringing of the cathedral bells on the hour of noon, for they have been silent since Thursday.[75] On one occasion the English Jockey Club amused its members by suspending huge effigies of Judas stuffed with copper coins before the clubhouse. At the proper time they were ignited and the members were privileged to watch the grimaces of the victims who had seized a hot copper. From these people the custom has been borrowed by the converted Yaqui Indians who have emigrated in part from Mexico to New Mexico. Thus, once a year the burning of Judas may yet be seen within the borders of the United States. Pictures of this may be found from time to time in the illustrated sections of the Sunday newspapers.

[74] See J. G. Frazer, *Balder the Beautiful*, I, 127-128. His authorities are F. Starr, "Holy Week in Mexico," *J. of Am. Folklore*, XII (1899), 164 ff.; C. B. Taylor, "Easter in Many Lands," *Everybody's Magazine*, 1903, p. 293. Another detailed description may be found in W. S. Walsh, *Curiosities of Popular Custom*, Philadelphia, 1898, pp. 581-582, but no authorities are cited. See further E. B. Tylor, *Anahuac*, London, 1861, p. 49, (mentioned by Andree, p. 253, n. 1); N. O. Winter, *Mexico and Her People of Today*, Boston, 1907, pp. 233-34; C. Sartorius, *Mexiko*, 1859, p. 258 (cited by Hoffmann-Krayer, *Schweizerisches Arch.f.Volksk.*, XI [1907], 246).

[75] On the custom of using rattles and the like during Holy Week instead of bells see an interesting article by Andree, "Ratschen, Klappern und das Verstummen der Karfreitagsglocken," *Zs. d. Ver.f. Volkskunde*, XX (1910), 250-264, and Sartori, *Sitte und Brauch*, VII, 139, n. 2. In Mexico City a huge wooden device something like a water-wheel is used at this time, see Andree, p. 253.

"Scenes of the same sort, though on a less ambitious scale, are witnessed," says Sir J. G. Frazer, "among the Catholics of South America on the same day (Easter Saturday). In Brazil the mourning for the death of Christ ceases at noon on Easter Saturday and gives place to an extravagant burst of joy at his resurrection. Shots are fired everywhere, and effigies of Judas are hung on trees or dragged about the streets, to be finally burned or otherwise destroyed. In the Indian villages scattered among the wild valleys of the Peruvian Andes figures of the traitor, made of pasteboard and stuffed with squibs and crackers, are hanged on gibbets before the door of the church on Easter Saturday. Fire is set to them, and while they crackle and explode, the Indians dance and shout for joy at the destruction of their hated enemy. Similarly at Rio Hacha, in Colombia, Judas is represented during Holy Week by life-sized effigies, and the people fire at them as if they were discharging a sacred duty."[76] On the island of Guadeloupe a similar custom was celebrated at least as late as 1885. Judas, represented by a small cask, was dragged about on Holy Thursday. When the cask had been beaten to pieces, the fragments were burned.[77]

In such variety, then, has the folk preserved the ancient custom of burning Judas. There is a certain curious, antiquarian interest in seeing in what differing ways it has maintained itself, how widely it has spread, and in noting that the very institution which attempted to defeat

---

[76] Frazer, *Balder the Beautiful*, I, 127-28. He cites the following authorities: K. von den Steinen, *Unter den Naturvölkern Zentralbrasiliens*, Berlin, 1894, pp. 458 ff.; E. Montet, "Religion et superstition dans l'Amerique du Sud," *Rev. de l'hist. des religions*, XXII (1895), 145; J. J. von Tschudi, *Peru: Reiseskizzen aus den Jahren 1838-42*, St. Gallen, 1846, II, 189 ff.; H. Candelier, *Rio Hacha et les Indiens Goajires*, Paris, 1893, p. 85. According to E. L. Urlin (*Festivals, Holy Days and Saints' Days*, London, 1915, p. 93) it is celebrated on Low Sunday, the Sunday after Easter, in Brazil.

[77] A. Corre, *Rev. des traditions populaires*, X (1895), 376.

the intent and to destroy the heathen connotation of the spring fires by bringing them into association with the traitor has itself propagated the rite, now thoroughly Christianized, in the New World. But there is more than casual amusement in thus tracing the history of the rite. Once more the passage of belief and custom from the upper strata of society to the lower is demonstrated. The Judas fires are an ecclesiastical substitute for the heathen ceremony; in them, where they are truly native, we have a foundation of an ancient, communal, pre-Christian rite on which has been erected a Christian superstructure. But the Bohemian custom, and still more obviously those reported from the New World, cannot have been of long standing. Frau Ohnefalsch-Richter, indeed, holds that the German customs have been transplanted from the Eastern Church and the Mediterranean. In the later instances we have a folk custom which owes its origin wholly to imitation. The folk does not create, but borrows. And in the course of time practises which were once entirely distinct in origin and purpose come to serve much the same end. Remnants of the former intent of the Judas fires are still to be discerned in the German customs. But the Easter uproar in the church and the reviling of the traitor's memory, which are certainly to be distinguished in their origins from the fires, have become an end in themselves.[78]

[78] Professor Hepding sends me this last reference when all is in type. In the villages of the Sauerland (Hesse) the boys and youths gather on the evening before Easter to chase Judas (*um den Judas zu jagen*). They try to keep awake by telling stories and riddles, but should any one fall asleep, his coat is nailed fast to the bench. At midnight, when the bell sounds, all stamp their feet, hammer the benches, swing the rattles, and rush out the door. The sleepy ones, too, spring up, but at the expense of their coats and jackets. See F. W. Grimme, *Das Sauerland und Seine Bewohner*[3], p. 163.

www.ingramcontent.com/pod-product-compliance
Lightning Source LLC
Chambersburg PA
CBHW071141090426

42736CB00012B/2192